# THE
# PEABODY

BY

Scott Faragher & Katherine Harrington

OPENS ABOUT FEBURARY 1, 1925

625 ROOMS

625 BATHS

TWO FLOORS SPECIALLY DESIGNED SAMPLE ROOMS

COPYRIGHT 2017 Scott Faragher & Katherine Harrington
ISBN: 978-0-9863726-7-4
Published by Death Cat Media, LLC
PO Box 50292
Nashville, TN. 37205
615-353-0573
Deathcatmedia.com
Email: deathcatmedia@gmail.com

**PEABODY HOTEL.**

**AMERICAN AND EUROPEAN PLAN,**

C. B. GALLOWAY & CO. Props.,

**MEMPHIS, TENN.**

**The 1925 Hotel Peabody shortly after its opening**

**CONTACT**
The Peabody
149 Union Avenue
Memphis, Tennessee 38103
Phone: 901-529-4000
FAX: 901-529-3600
Toll Free Reservations: 1-800-PEABODY
Website: peabodymemphis.com

PEABODY HOTEL

## FIRST THINGS FIRST

If you're thinking about visiting Memphis for a weekend getaway, or having a social event, such as a class reunion, wedding, business meeting or convention, the first thing you should do is visit The Peabody's excellent website. Here you will find helpful information including room rates, and special offers, as well as photos of various rooms and suites. **peabodymemphis.com**

## TIMELINE

**1869** On Feb 5, the 1st Peabody Hotel opened at Main & Monroe.

**1872** Russian Grand Duke Alexis, son of Czar Alexander II visited the Peabody.

**1873** The Panic of 1873 negatively affected the financial well-being of the United States, and also Memphis.

**1901** President William McKinley attended the Confederate Reunion, the largest gathering in the city's history.

**1904** Telephones were installed in many of the hotel's guest rooms.

**1906** On July 15, at 4:30 am, part of the 1st first Peabody Hotel collapsed destroying twenty-four rooms and the kitchen.

**1907** The Memphis Hotel Company was formed to operate the Peabody Hotel.

**1923** The first Peabody Hotel closed for good on August 28, 1923.

**1925** The 2nd Hotel Peabody opened at its present location on September 1st with an invitation only grand preview celebration. The Hotel Peabody officially opened to the public the following morning.

**1925** Hoyt Wooten, founder of what would later become WREC Radio and WREC TV, opened a retail radio shop at the Hotel Peabody and was one of the hotel's earliest lobby shop owners.

**1929** WREC Radio Station opened new $25,000 studio in the basement of the Hotel Peabody.

**1932** Prince Theodore Romanov, nephew of Czar Nicholas II visited the Peabody.

**1935** The new Samovar Room opened for the 1935 Nite-Cap season.

**1936** The Cadet Room replaced the Samovar for the 1936 Nite-Cap season, and was opened by George Hamilton's Music Box Orchestra.

**1937** CBS Radio began broadcasting WREC Radio's live big band broadcasts.

**1939** The enclosed Skyway opened on the roof on January 20.

**1940** WREC opened a larger $60,000 studio in the basement of the Hotel Peabody.

**1948** In June, Jack and Marilyn Belz celebrated held their wedding reception at The Peabody, unaware, that their own history would ever, let alone forever, be intertwined with the hotel's.

**1952** A four year long program of fully air conditioning the hotel was completed.

**1953** The Alsonett hotel chain bought the Peabody in July for $7,495,000.

**1956** On January 1, WREC TV Channel 3 began broadcasting from its new television studio in the basement of the hotel.

**1965** The Peabody was sold at public auction on the courthouse Steps, a victim of suburban migration.

**1968** The completely restored Peabody had a grand reopening as the Sheraton-Peabody on March 7.

**1972** With the Peabody again for sale, WREC-TV, now known as WREG-TV, began seeking another location.

**1974** The Peabody was purchased by James Lane in January for $1,078,000. It was immediately reopened but closed on April 1 the same year.

**1975** On July 31, The Peabody was again sold on the steps of the Courthouse at a public auction. Real estate mogul Jack Belz became the hotel's new owner.

**1977** In September, The Peabody was placed on the National Register of Historic Places, a distinction it still holds.

**1978** In July, in excess of 1,800 people lined the street alongside The Peabody hoping for an opportunity to buy a memento from the Peabody as its beds, TVs, glassware, linens, tablecloths, and other items were sold to the public.

**1981** On September 21, the completely restored Peabody reopened, 56 years to the day after its original Grand Opening in 1925.

**2002** In September 2002 WREG-TV opened a new studio in Peabody Place.

Hotel Peabody
Memphis

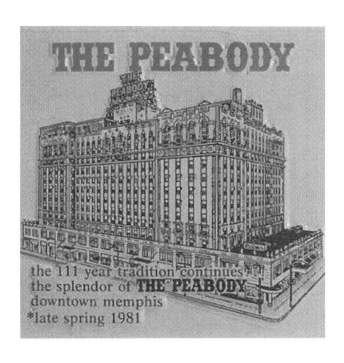

THE PEABODY

the 111 year tradition continues*
the splendor of THE PEABODY
downtown memphis
*late spring 1981

The history of The Peabody has truly been intertwined with that of the city of Memphis since 1869. Today, the mention of Memphis immediately causes one to automatically think of The Peabody Hotel.

Since 1925, The Peabody sign, whether as the Peabody Hotel, the Hotel Peabody, Sheraton Peabody, or The Peabody, has announced the presence of `The South's Grand Hotel.'

# PREFACE

It is normally stated that a building is simply a structure that can be architecturally attractive or unattractive, but it is basically a combination of bricks, stone, concrete, wood, paint, etc. In truth, a building is much more than that. There are certain great buildings in the world which are symbols of countries. These include capitols, The White House, Buckingham Palace, The Kremlin. There are other buildings such as The Peabody which represent a certain period in architecture and excellence of design and quality building materials. But much more than that, a repository of memories. The Peabody in Memphis is a treasure which is enjoyed by millions of people and is remembered with nostalgia for past graduations, weddings, proms, dinners, roof top dancing, its extraordinary lobby, youth, maturity, age-a place where you relive old memories and make new ones.

When my parents, of blessed memory, Philip and Sarah Belz were to be married, they tried unsuccessfully to have the event at The Peabody, but it was booked. Almost all of the social events of great significance to my wife and me (and countless others), took place at The Peabody Hotel. This included our own wedding reception in the Continental Ballroom, which we remember almost as yesterday, even though it was nearly 70 years ago. Since our marriage, countless thousands of people have similarly made new memories which they relive constantly when visiting `their Peabody.'

When we acquired The Peabody, it was a very sad moment in the history of our city. It was not too many years after the tragic assassination of Dr. Martin Luther King, no more than about a mile from The Peabody. There was a general real estate recession. The ravages of the rampages that followed the assassination in the form of boarded up stores and the accelerating exodus of offices from downtown had left many businesses foreclosed and shuttered. The Peabody was among them. When we acquired it, most had concluded that it should be razed because it was an architectural dinosaur, a relic of the past, but not the future. Each time we visited and toured it, we became more and more in love with it, and resolved that it would not be torn down, but rather, would be renewed and brought back to a condition far nicer than it ever was in its heyday. We are gratified-more than that-overjoyed, that we have been blessed with the resolve and ability to accomplish that and even more. We've added to the hotel. We have continuously improved it and refined it as one does in cutting and polishing a fine diamond. In addition, early on we knew that we had to do more than simply reopen The Peabody, but to create a new centrality in downtown, the reverberations from which would help energize the redevelopment of our downtown, and even the enlargement of it. All of this has and is occurring and was already in play as the new millennium came.

The Peabody Place project is an eight block development extending from The Peabody to Beale St. and from the waterfront eastwardly to almost Danny Thomas Blvd. It is now open and drawing many thousands a day with the great variety of opportunities for living, working, entertaining, exercising, and general enjoyment. Now on the scene is Mud Island with its many award winning residential communities, the rebuilt South Bluffs, with exquisite river view homes, a vibrant St. Jude Hospital and Research Center growing daily, the expanded Convention Center, the AutoZone Ballpark, and now the new NBA Arena. These are only some of the many elements of the reemerging and vibrant downtown which has become again-and forever-the cultural, financial and entertainment capital of the Mid-South-and always with its crown jewel, The Peabody, at its center.

Jack Belz

# On Historic Preservation

It's worth mentioning that a civilization is in many cases ultimately defined by its architecture, and sadly, much of the American architecture of the past is in danger. Considering what has been lost already, buildings, homes, and even warehouse structures from the late 1800s and early 1900s have become increasingly significant, and rare. Recently in Nashville, for example three of the few remaining 1920s mansions on West End were razed simultaneously without notice. They'd been there as long as anyone currently living could remember, and then one day they simply weren't there. Already they are being replaced with newer, more 'eco-friendly' and energy efficient multiunit boxes which resemble other multiunit residential boxes on the same side of the street. Sadly, progress is often no respecter of architecture.

During the early development of American cities, if some former landmark, or even some old residence or building which had outlived its original purpose was destroyed in the name of progress, it wasn't necessarily that important. Whatever came along to replace it would most likely probably be even better. This was generally true through the 1930s, but with some exceptions, the architecture of today, both residential and commercial has degenerated in favor of cost effectiveness. Gone are the ornate stone carvings and marble columns of yesteryear, replaced by cement blocks, chrome, glass, and hideous aluminum or vinyl siding.

While much has been lost in Memphis, there have been some unlikely rescues recently, including the Nineteenth Century Club on Union (a former residence), and the Chisca Hotel, a downtown landmark, both of which were unlikely survivors. The resurrection of the Chisca can in large measure be credited to the revival of the surrounding area, including Main Street in particular, itself a beneficiary of the revival of Beale Street and the downtown area in general. Ultimately this rebirth of downtown Memphis must be attributed specifically to the restoration of The Peabody itself, and to the realization of the long term vision behind that undertaking. I know of no other city in America where the name of a city automatically calls to mind the name of a hotel and vice versa, but indeed, Memphis and The Peabody are synonymous.

It is important that individuals become actively involved in the effort to save what's left. To that end, we urge you to join whatever organizations exist in your own cities which endeavor to preserve the physical remnants of our common heritage. They can always use volunteers, money, and the strength of numbers.

In Memphis, there is Memphis Heritage, Inc., a nonprofit organization dedicated to historic preservation. Their website is www.memphisheritage.org Check it out.

Scott Faragher & Katherine Harrington

This postcard shows what it lists as the first hotel in Memphis 'before the war,' which even now, in the South, means the Civil War, or the War Between the States, depending on one's sympathies. Regrettably the name of the hotel and its location are not mentioned.

## INTRODUCTION

The History of The Peabody Hotel while very interesting, is fairly cut and dry in terms of certain memorable dates, but much information about other Memphis Hotels of the period is not as clear. Our sources as authors for the information presented herein are from a variety of places, including personal knowledge, period press articles, reference books, and personal interviews. But some of the especially early dates and data regarding other early Memphis hotels are conflicting. For example, there is Joseph Isele's brief work entitled 'The History of Memphis Hotels from 1823 to 1929.' Isele and his brothers owned or leased several hotels in the early days of Memphis, including the original Peabody, so his information should be accurate. Regarding the former Claridge Hotel, for example, he notes that it was built in 1922 on the former site of the Arlington. He then says on the same page, two paragraphs later, that the Arlington Hotel opened on June 1, 1924. He also states that the Claridge Hotel had 557 rooms, while on the back of a period postcard of the Claridge, it says that it has 400 rooms. Dates vary from source to source as well. Did the original Gayoso open in 1842 or 1843, for example? I mention this only so that the reader will not consider any reference to Memphis hotels other than The Peabody to be definitive. This is rather an attempt to provide the interested reader with an accurate and informative history of Memphis' most famous landmark, the Peabody Hotel. The inclusion of other hotels of the same or earlier periods serves merely as a backdrop for the interest of the reader. Memphis still has several large hotels remaining from the 1920s such as the Parkview, now a retirement home, the Chisca, currently under restoration, the Claridge, and Wm. Len, now apartment buildings, and of course, The Peabody, the only one of the great Memphis hotels still serving in its original capacity. Other, older hotels Such as the Marquette, Forest Park, Plaza Hotel, The King Cotton, the Arlington, and others, though once successful, are now gone altogether and largely forgotten.

The Peabody in Memphis is known worldwide for its famous marble fountain and swimming ducks. And while it is the ducks which immediately come to mind when The Peabody Hotel is mentioned, the hotel is really most famous for its history and long tradition of magnificent and elegant service. Most people assume that the grand Peabody Hotel at Second and Union is the original Peabody Hotel. Considering its massive size and imposing presence, it's easy to understand why. It looks like something which has always been there. For all but a few Memphians, and indeed for most Americans, it is The Peabody Hotel. But the current Peabody, first built in 1925, is actually Memphis' second Peabody Hotel, and has its roots in an earlier structure which was built in 1869. Beginning with the year, 2000 and the new millennium, it can be said that The Peabody has its footprints planted in three centuries.

**The 1ˢᵗ Peabody Hotel**

# Peabody Hotel,

CORNER MAIN & MONROE STS.,

## MEMPHIS, - TENNESSEE.

This Hotel is now opened, and will be kept in Style
equal to any in the country, by

## D. COCKRELL & SONS,

Who have been long and favorably known as the Proprietors of the GAYOSO HOUSE, of this City.

There is connected with the House,

### A MODEL BILLIARD HALL,

With eight of Phelan's Elegant Tables.

The 1st Peabody was one of several early Memphis hotels. It was noted for its luxurious interior appointments, a tradition which was maintained and expanded upon at the current 1925 Peabody. The hotel is similar in appearance to Nashville's Maxwell House (1859-1961) As you can see in this 1905 postcard photograph, there was already an established practice of hotels renting retail space to businesses of all types in areas surrounding the hotel lobby on the main floor, and on the outside edges of the mezzanine in larger hotels. These businesses included everything from cigar and newspaper stands to optometrists, physicians, dentists, drug stores, and liquor and package stores. Merchants of all types, offered a variety of dry goods catering to hotel guests, a practice which still exists today at many historic hotels, including The Peabody.

The use of retail commercial space was beneficial to all parties involved, as hotel patrons in many instances did not have to wander around a possibly unfamiliar downtown area looking for something which was available at the hotel. The hotel benefitted from the increased income from the rental of retail spaces.

**Nashville's 1859 Maxwell House Hotel** was considered by some to have been similar in appearance to the first Peabody Hotel. Both were in the heart of downtown, both were five stories tall, and each noted for luxurious appointments, first class service, attention to guests, and great food. The Maxwell House burned in 1961.

**The original 1869 Peabody Hotel** is shown with the larger, steel framed section at the left, a later addition. Its design was simple and visually appealing.

**The original Peabody opened in 1869** at the intersection of Main and Monroe. The portion of the hotel shown at the left side of this image is indicative of the trend toward taller buildings in prosperous downtown areas. In fact, the text on this postcard proclaimed the Peabody Hotel to be 'In the Heart of the Business, Shopping, and Skyscraper District of the City.' The cars pictured here appear to be from the early 1920s. Note the prominent fire escape ladders at the left of the newer section. As time passed, fire escapes would eventually be enclosed within hotels at strategic points, ultimately eliminating unsightly external stairs which were subject to corrosion and rust due to continual exposure to the elements.

The Peabody Hotel's name would over time change from Peabody Hotel, to Hotel Peabody, and finally The Peabody. This additional image is included to show the new skyscraper in the background. It's worth mentioning that Memphis had 'money' before Nashville did, despite the fact that Nashville was an older city. Interestingly, the basic design of Memphis was laid out by John Overton and Andrew Jackson, two Nashvillians. Memphis benefitted from the cotton trade as well as from its prime location on the bluffs of the Mississippi River, a major thoroughfare. As a consequence of its wealth the downtown area developed more quickly than Nashville's after the Civil War.

By the end of the first decade of the 20th Century, Memphis was outpacing Nashville, the state capitol. The 1895 D.T. Porter Building was considered the city's first skyscraper, but Memphis had others as well, such as the 1904 Memphis Trust Building, and the Bank of Commerce tower. Memphis had the tallest building in the state of Tennessee with the magnificently beautiful 29 story, 1930 Sterick Building until the mid-1950s when Nashville's ultramodern Life & Casualty Building opened, besting the Bluff City's tallest building, by a whopping one story. Despite the loss of significant architecture in its downtown area, during the 1970s and 1980s, the extent of what remains in Memphis residentially, from prior to 1940, is indicative of its early prosperity even now. Memphis, like Nashville had its most significant residential architecture as close to the downtown area as possible. This was a matter of convenience in the horse and buggy days, but as the era of the automobile arrived, and the downtown business area expanded, many elaborate downtown residences were destroyed as department stores, restaurants, and hotels took their places. This was a national phenomenon and applied to most large, rapidly growing US cities.

The first Peabody Hotel was named in honor of philanthropist

George Peabody by the hotel's builder Robert Campbell Brinkley, a lawyer and businessman, who'd moved From Nashville to Memphis in 1842. As the story is told, Brinkley was on his way to England in search of a loan to aid his troubled railroad when he met the famous George Peabody aboard ship. They developed a friendship and Peabody subsequently helped Brinkley get his railroad back on track. With his finances secure, Brinkley turned his attention to the creation of a grand hotel in Memphis, to be called Brinkley House. According to legend, its name was changed to the Peabody Hotel upon Brinkley hearing the news of Peabody's death (London, November 4, 1869), but this is unlikely, since the original Peabody Hotel opened on February 5, 1869, as the Peabody Hotel, basically ten months before Peabody's death. With much fanfare, the Peabody Hotel opened Main and Monroe, with a grand celebration attended by 200 of the city's most prominent couples. The Memphis *Daily Post* reported the evening's festivities the following day, as follows:

"Mine generous hosts Cockrell and sons of the Peabody Hotel gave a grand ball to their patrons and guests last night which fulfilled their long standing reputation of being the champions in all matters relating to dancing and feasting. Every member of the brilliant throng which graced the spacious and elegant hall last night was as sure of an unbounded enjoyment when preparing for the occasion as when in fullness of his fruition, the appearance of the morning light admonished him to retire from the joys of night to his bed and take a moment's rest."

**George Peabody** (Circa. 1850)

The well-known name of financier George Peabody is especially significant in the state of Tennessee, both in Memphis and Nashville. In Memphis, there is of course The Peabody Hotel but there is also a major thoroughfare named in his honor, as well as George Peabody Park. In Nashville there is a Peabody Street, but more significantly the George Peabody College for Teachers, now a part of the Vanderbilt University system was named in his honor and founded with his donations. George Peabody is usually referred to simply as a `philanthropist' and that's as far as it goes. But since his name graces the subject of this book something more should be said about him. George Peabody was born in Massachusetts in 1795 and began working as a youth at a local dry goods store. He moved to Washington, D.C., then to Baltimore. He moved to London, England in 1837 and established George Peabody & Company where he became extremely successful in dealing with financial matters between various American and English companies. Most of his large fortune was spent in charitable and philanthropic endeavors including funds which either created or supported a number of projects. Among them were the George Peabody College for Teachers in Nashville, the Peabody Institute of Baltimore, the Peabody Museum of Natural History at Yale, and the Peabody Museum of Archaeology and Ethnology at Harvard, among others.

Most significant was his establishment of the Peabody Fund in 1867 to further education in the war torn South. Peabody died in London on November 4, 1869.

Many post Civil War hotels in major cities throughout the nation opened with pomp and circumstance, and such was the case with the original Peabody Hotel. In the early days of American hotels, luxuries were few. Indeed, nearly all of the modern amenities which the American traveler of today takes for granted were rarely available, even in the best hotels prior to the War Between the States. Even after the war, few hotels had private bathrooms. Bathrooms were usually found, one or two per floor at the end of the hall. Hotels were generally cold in the winter and hot in the summer, with little of the creature comforts provided by modern engineering. There were also problems with fire and natural gas, and hotels of the period were frequently destroyed by fire, and many travelers died simply trying to get a good night's sleep. Consequently, when the original Peabody Hotel opened with 75 individual rooms, each with its own private bathroom, it was considered luxurious. The $60,000 hotel also contained a saloon, a ballroom, and a lobby. Room prices during this initial period were $4 per day and included meals, a practice which sadly no longer exists. Gas lights and open fires in the room's fireplace cost extra as they did in most hotels of the day. In fact a 1934 article in the Memphis *Press Scimitar* related the following:

"John T. Wilkinson of the National Bank of Commerce has a bill which Alfred D. Carter, Marion, Ark., found in some old papers recently. It bears the date of Feb. 2, 1869 when the Peabody was then at Main and Monroe, and was owned by D. Cockrell & Sons. It showed that Mrs. P.A. Cox owed the hotel $28 for one week's board, $14 for her child's board, $1.75 for gas, and $3.00 for `fire in the room' making a total of $46.75 for the week."

This is curious in that the opening date of the first Peabody is recorded and reported as February 5, 1869. On the other hand, as with the 1924 Arlington Hotel in Hot Springs, the Peabody Hotel likely opened earlier than its official grand opening in order to make certain that the staff were fully trained, and that everything ran smoothly and was in proper order before the big day.

Also, Col. D. Cockrell was the first manager of the Peabody, and not its owner. He was well experienced in the operation and management of hotels, having been the manager of the magnificent Memphis Gayoso in its pre-Civil War days.

**The lobby of the first Peabody** was as magnificent as it was massive. The beautiful woodwork and stenciling represented the height of elegance, establishing a precedent which would be continued with the current 1925 structure.

**Lobby of the First Peabody (alternate view).** The arched doorways gave the lobby a Moorish feel. The spacious open mezzanine is a long-standing tradition in luxury hotels.

**First Peabody Hotel letterhead.**

B.S. Parker was the Peabody Hotel's resident manager when this letterhead was in use. In old hotels, especially before telephones, the manager generally handled all reservation requests in writing.

**Another view of the lobby**

**1913 Egg Cup**

This 1913 egg cup is from Wieden, Germany company Bauscher, which also had offices in Chicago and New York, at least prior to World War I, which means this was from the first, 1869 Peabody at its original location on Main & Monroe. Most first class hotels Generally had their own china, as did the later, 1925 second Hotel Peabody.

So Robert Brinkley, with the earlier help of George Peabody, had succeeded in creating a grand and modern hotel for this prosperous postwar Southern city, a hotel which would serve well into the next century. For some reason, within less than a year after the successful Peabody Hotel's grand opening, Col. Brinkley gave the hotel to his daughter, Annie Overton Brinkley, as a wedding gift, upon her marriage to Robert Snowden.

The Peabody, like other major hotels of the late 1800s served not only as a social center, with lavish parties and celebrations, but also functioned as a business center. Memphis had fortunately survived much of the destruction visited upon other parts of the South during the Civil War, like Atlanta, Vicksburg, and Columbia, South Carolina, for example, and was therefore ready to move proudly forward into the 20th Century. But not quite yet. For despite its sophistication at many levels, Memphis was, during the immediate postwar years, still a rough and untamed river city. While socially the city possessed the upper classes of the cotton and sugar based plantation systems, there were also the hard and tough frontiersmen for which Tennessee was noted. Add the large number of ex-Confederates, carpetbaggers, some legitimate northern businessmen, and the large number of newly freed former slaves, and the mix was eclectic, to say the least. The 1870s were an interesting and often violent time for Memphis, and the Peabody Saloon and Billiard Parlor, as well as the hotel itself were hotbeds of gambling and other vices, and not all of the hotel's retail tenants were of the highest caliber. During this period The Peabody housed traveling salesmen, tradeshows, gamblers, fortune tellers, psychics, crooks, card sharks, and hucksters of all kinds. Real and self-proclaimed doctors and hucksters sold phony medicinal cures, as well as riverboat gamblers. Anyone even remotely familiar with Memphis and The Peabody has heard the expression 'Plantations were won and lost there on a roll of the dice.' This was probably no exaggeration since Cotton was King, Memphis was its capital, and the Peabody Hotel was its social center and headquarters. While wedding parties have always been a popular tradition at hotels people of today do not, as a rule, think of hotels when considering funeral arrangements, funerals at hotels were common during this period, and the original Peabody had its share.

By 1876 the Peabody was again in the hands of its original owner, Robert Brinkley, who hired C. Galloway, former Chief of staff at the Gayoso as the Peabody's new manager.

While Memphis had survived reconstruction better than some parts of the South, Memphis, like nearby Holly Springs, Mississippi, and New Orleans, downriver was ravaged by the Yellow Fever epidemic. It hit Memphis in August, 1878. There was an immediate mass exodus with half the population leaving the city. All of the hotels closed with the exception of the Peabody, whose new manager Galloway, served both the Peabody and the city well despite having survived yellow fever himself. More than a hundred doctors and several hundred nurses who'd been brought to help fight yellow fever had been lodged at the Peabody during the epidemic.

The history of the Peabody Hotel, as connected with that of the city of Memphis, is a tradition started with the original hotel, as noted above. Local newspapers of the time, such as the *Daily Post*, and the *Public Ledger*, eagerly noted when famous citizens such as Nathan Bedford Forrest, Robert E. Lee, President Andrew Johnson, and other important citizens of the era visited Memphis and stayed at the Peabody. The first hotel was frequently the site of many significant social events as well, including balls, dinners, and gatherings of the Memphis bon ton. Perhaps the most famous of all its festivities was the Memphis reunion of Confederate soldiers in 1901. On this occasion, the original Peabody served as the headquarters for this historic veterans' reunion which brought in excess of 165,000 former Confederate soldiers to the city.

Despite hopes to the contrary, the bright promise of the postwar future for Memphis was not to be realized until after the 1870s. By the end of the decade, however, Memphis had emerged once again, ready to take its place as one of the South's most important cities. The Peabody Hotel with newly added electric lights and an external iron fire escape, remained the business and social center of Memphis, just as it had since its inception. But trouble for the famed hotel was literally just around the corner.

With the electronic and magnetic hotel keys of the present, actual physical keys are now a thing of the past. Original hotel keys were metal with the room number engraved on the surface of each key. The key was affixed to a fob making it easy to locate. These fobs were generally made of brass, and sometimes nickel plated, specific to each hotel, and usually very artistic. This rare brass key fob from the first Peabody Hotel features the image of George Peabody on one side and a depiction of the first Peabody Hotel on the opposite side. It's difficult to precisely date this item. It shows the newer steel addition, which was added after 1906, so that places it after 1906, but before 1925, when the current Peabody Hotel opened. Hotel keys are quite collectible now and some of them are relatively expensive.

**The above Key fobs are original to the 1925 Peabody. They were nickel plated brass or bronze. In most of those which remain, the nickel has worn off over time.**

This aluminum alloy was very lightweight and was probably the last of the metal key fobs. While still interesting, it is a far cry from its two predecessors. By the time this fob was in use there was an inscription on the back which read 'Drop in any mailbox. Return Postage Guaranteed.' Ultimately most hotels switched to generic plastic fobs, all of which looked inexpensive, and were.

**Ballroom or Banquet Hall.** After the Civil War, Memphis recovered faster than many other Southern cities, and the first Peabody Hotel (1869) was in its day, a social and business center of post war Memphis. This spacious area would accommodate a large crowd for either meetings, dances, banquets or other social gatherings. Note the marble floor and the architectural details of the ceiling and arches.

This discount card is from the first hotel and is dated 1898. It entitles the bearer to a discount as stated: `...is entitled to a discount of fifty cents a day on the American Plan, on all rooms for which the price is $2.50 per day and upwards, and 25 cents a day on the European Plan, on all rooms for which the price is $1.00 per day and upwards; and when accompanied by his wife, the price for her shall be the same.'

The first Peabody's main dining room is shown through one of the many Moorish style arches surrounding the mezzanine.

**A broader view of the same restaurant**. Presumably the framed portrait on the far wall is that of George Peabody.

**Hotels of the period served a variety of functions. Here, to the right, are ticket offices for Consolidated, and the Illinois Central Railroad.**

Memphis had always boasted a number of hotels since its earliest days. Joseph Isele in his paper 'The History Of Memphis Hotels from 1823 to 1929' mentions that Memphis' first hotel was the Old Bell Tavern which was built in 1823, and was located on Front Street. Other hotels quickly followed as the city's population increased from an estimated fifty people in 1820. By 1830 the

Clark House was operating at the corner of Main and Winchester. By the early 1840s, Memphis had a half dozen first class hotels, including the City Hotel, the Exchange Hotel, and the Johnson Hotel. In 1843, according to Isele, the Gayoso House opened and was 'one of the most spacious and elegant hotels in the Western Country.' By the mid-1850s some of the earlier hotels had disappeared and others had taken their places, among them were the United States Hotel, the Apium House, the Arlington, Bostick House, the Commercial House, the Wharf Boat Hotel, the Overton Hotel, and the Washington House which advertised board and lodging for $1.00 per day.

**The Mezzanine level** offered a place for visiting or tables for writing.

**Interior view of first hotel.** Probably Mezzanine level.

During the 1880s the main hotels in Memphis were the Peabody, the Gaston, the Fransioli, the Clarendon, the Luehrman, and the Duffy Hotel. Despite the presence of many hotels in Memphis, The Peabody's chief competitor had always been the Gayoso. The Gayoso opened in February 1843, burned, was rebuilt, and reopened in 1858, and again closed on April 2, 1868, prior to the opening of the Peabody in 1869. The Gayoso reopened but succumbed to a fire again on June 28, 1879. By 1896 the Gayoso was in receivership, and was bought in 1898 for $81,000. The Gayoso, like so many hotels of the period, succumbed to fire again on July 4, 1899 in 'one of the most spectacular fires of the period.' Once again, the Peabody reigned supreme. But the Gayoso was not prepared to be counted out just yet, and another, all new Gayoso was constructed, which opened in 1902.

**This circa 1895 photo** shows the first Peabody at its prime as an integral part of the downtown Memphis business district. The awnings, mostly raised in this image, were functional rather than ornamental, and could be lowered as needed, keeping sun, glare, and heat out of store front windows, and rain off of patrons.

On January1, 1906, The Isele Brothers, local hotel owners who had operated the Arlington Hotel, leased the Peabody from its owners at a rental cost of $25,000 per year and took charge of its operation. On July 15, 1906, at 4:30 a.m., part of the Peabody collapsed, destroying 24 rooms as well as the kitchen. As a result of the destruction the Isele Brothers were released from their lease and an all new 200 room addition was built, at a cost of $350,000. It was the first steel structure erected in Memphis. In 1907 The Memphis Hotel Company was formed which owned and operated the hotel.

**The original Hotel Gayoso** opened in 1843, burned, was rebuilt, reopened in 1858, closed in 1868, reopened, burned again in 1879, was rebuilt again, and burned once more in 1899.

**The lobby of the 1902** Gayoso in a somewhat later photograph.

**A new Gayoso Hotel was constructed in 1902 which was newer and larger than the 1869 Peabody.** The new 300 room Hotel Gayoso billed itself as 'The South's Most Aristocratic Hotel,' offered what it considered to be reasonable rates, and was described in advertising as 'Famous for Years,' which it was.

The population of Memphis had increased rapidly from the slightly more than 20,000 at the end of the Civil War, to around 100,000 by 1900. This was an astounding growth in such a short period of a mere 35 years, especially so in light of the fact that half the city's population fled the city in 1878 to escape yellow fever. The construction boom which paralleled this population increase produced many of Memphis' finest buildings, including some of the South's first skyscrapers. Hotel construction also soared, and within a short span of time, newer, larger, and more magnificent hotels made their debut.

The new million dollar Chisca Hotel opened in 1913 at Main and Linden, with `400 bright outside rooms' and `Homelike Southern Cooking.' Outside rooms were certainly desirable in the stagnant summer heat of Memphis. Additionally, the view of the city afforded by outside rooms was desirable, permitting guests with higher level rooms to look out upon the city and the Mississippi River. Like the present Peabody Hotel, and most grand hotels of the time, the Chisca featured an elegant open lobby and mezzanine.

**The 1913 Hotel Chisca.**

**The Chisca Plaza** annex is seen here in the early 1960s. By this period many motorists preferred the convenience, modernity, and less formal atmosphere of older, grand hotels. Newer additions, often known as a hotel's 'Motor Lodge' kept some downtown hotels competitive, for a time. Another Tennessee example was the historic Read House in Chattanooga which offered a newer motor lodge addition. The Read House survived, the Chisca did not. The Chisca had been boarded and vacant for decades, but fortunately has been under renovation for several years and now houses several retail businesses as restoration continues.

Memphis was booming and more new hotels were on the horizon. The Civil War and reconstruction, to the extent that it existed in Memphis, were behind them, as was the Yellow Fever epidemic. The Memphis Hotel Company (1907) owned and operated the Gayoso and the Peabody, but would also own the new 400 room Chisca, the three most important hotels in downtown Memphis

This advertisement was placed after 1913 when the 400 room
Chisca opened, but before 1925 when the new Peabody opened.

But suburban expansion was well underway by the early 1960s, and ultimately many downtown hotels suffered as a result. This, in conjunction with the development of the Interstate system further hurt downtown areas as it became possible to bypass some urban areas altogether, and stay in new and inexpensive motels and hotels at Interstate exits. In the 1920s, this was all in the future and couldn't be foreseen, so let's return to the 1920s.

Other downtown hotels followed the Chisca in the 1920s. The George Vincent opened at 855 Union. The elegant 16 story, 400 room, 400 bath Hotel Claridge opened in 1924 at 109 North Main. The Hotel De Voy at 69 Jefferson Street overlooking Confederate Park, opened in 1925 before being renamed the King Cotton. The eight story, 200 room, 200 bath, Hotel Tennessee opened in 1927 at 3rd and Union, literally across the street from the present Peabody. The magnificent Parkview, and William Len Hotels, also appeared in Memphis during the years between 1920 and 1930.

**The Claridge**

## The Claridge

The large and elegant 400 room Claridge, like the Peabody, and Parkview Hotels, was noted for its outdoor roof area, which in the case of the Claridge was known as the Magnolia Roof Gardens. Orchestras and nightly dancing were featured on the roof or in the famous Balinese Room. It was built on the site of the former Arlington Hotel in 1922 at a cost of $1,550,000. It opened in 1924, and billed itself as `Memphis' Finest Hotel.' By 1950 all rooms had private baths and were air conditioned.

**The Hotel De Voy**                **Hotel King Cotton**

**The 1925 Hotel De Voy** built overlooking Confederate Park, and the Mississippi River offered `...safety and comfort without extravagance.' The Hotel De Voy was later renamed the King Cotton, and became part of the Alsonett chain. It survived for a time, but eventually fell to the wrecking ball in the early 1980s and became the site of the Morgan Keegan building. Alsonett also owned The Peabody 1953-1965.

**The King Cotton Hotel's dining room**

**The lobby of the King Cotton** was a far cry from that of The Peabody, but was spacious nonetheless. By the late 1970s, downtown Memphis hotels had largely been abandoned in favor of newer, less expensive, more modern chain motels, often located away from downtown areas. The rise of the interstate system, and cessation pf passenger rail service didn't help downtown hotels.

**The 1924 Parkview** on Poplar Ave. was one of several grand hotels which preceded the current 1925 Peabody. Its location, several miles away from downtown, placed it too far from the main business district and the train station at a time when nearly everything of commercial significance was fairly close to the river. Ultimately, the Parkview became a residential hotel, then apartments, and finally a retirement home, as it remains today. It was successful for a long time and, like the Peabody, was known for its elegant lobby and roof top dances.

The Peabody, which had long served as the city's social and business hub was past its prime. The original structure, was inadequate for the elegance and level of service the public had now come to expect, not just from the Peabody, but from hotels in general. In short, the original Peabody could no longer compete with the newer and more modern hotels which Memphis now boasted. Its greatest competitor was the Gayoso which despite its several fires had replaced the Peabody as the social and business center of the city by 1886. By 1896, however, the Gayoso was in receivership, but in 1902 an all new Gayoso was up and running, and the new 1913 Chisca was the talk of the town.

Ownership of the Peabody passed to the Memphis Hotel Company, operated by Robert Brinkley Snowden, a great grandson of Robert Campbell Brinkley, the man who built the first Peabody. The original Peabody closed its doors for good on August 28, 1923 without great fanfare or excitement, despite already announced plans for a new and grander Peabody. There was no joy, among those who gathered in remembrance there on its last night, and its passing truly marked the end of an era. The *Commercial Appeal* described it as "…a stark, silent sentinel, forming a grim, almost sinister silhouette against a star studded sky. It loomed over busy thoroughfares below, calmly awaiting its doom." The Peabody had been erected in the horse and buggy days when the streets were of packed dirt, and public transportation had consisted solely of horse-drawn trolleys. The historic hotel had seen the dawn of electricity, witnessed the birth of electric trolleys which ran on steel rails, paved streets, and the birth of the automobile, airplane, and other significant events. It had survived the yellow fever epidemic, World War I, and had prospered, and now it was to close. Many old timers openly wondered if Memphis would ever be the same. The hotel would be razed at a cost of $40,000.

But plans for the new hotel were already underway, and by the fall of 1923, the same year of its closing, construction had started on an all new Peabody Hotel, to be located at a different site. It would be owned by the Memphis Hotel Company, with former Gayoso manager Albert Parker in charge of the new Peabody construction project. Many architectural plans were submitted, but the final design selected and approved by the board of directors was that of Chicago architect Walter Ahlschlager. Thomas H. Allen of Memphis would serve as consulting engineer, and J. W. Hull Plumbing & Heating Contractors, also of Memphis would undertake the monumental task of heating and plumbing the new structure.

The bond department of the Bank of Commerce & Trust Company offered the following in regard to the new Hotel Peabody:

"This building to be erected on the block fronting 324 feet on Union Avenue, extending from Second to Third Streets, and running 200 feet to a new street to be known as Hotel Place. The hotel, to be known as the Hotel Peabody, is to be erected and equipped at an estimated cost of $4,000,000.00. It is to be mortgaged to secure an issue of $2,000,000.00 First Mortgage SIX PERCENT Sinking Fund Gold Bonds."

The above postcard from Chicago's Kurt Teich preceded the opening of the hotel and was no doubt sent in large quantities to potential tenants of office spaces as well as to known guests of the major Memphis hotels of the era.

MEMPHIS-The best city in the Southland- with the completion of the new Hotel Peabody, will offer the Commercial Traveler, the Business Man, the out of town Shopper and the Tourist the best hotel accommodations and service of any city in the South.

Caption from back of above postcard.

**The New Peabody Hotel, 1925.** This early photo of the new Hotel Peabody shortly after its opening clearly indicates its immense size. It was an impressive and massive architectural masterpiece, a timeless expression of form and function.

The building designed by Ahlschlager was a massive twelve story Italian Renaissance structure with terra cotta exterior detailing and an open 85 x 125 ft., two story lobby which is the center point of the hotel's interior. It was described as follows in a newspaper article from the period:

"The decorative scheme of the lobby is 18th century, South Italian. The room rises through two floors with huge square columns supporting the mezzanine balcony. The ceiling is beamed in polychrome and frames two large and very beautiful art glass skylights. A gold railing extends entirely around the mezzanine promenade and the base of it all around has a strip of walnut wood.

In the center of the lobby is the fountain, carved out of a block of travertine marble."

The back of this postcard reads 'Summer and winter air-conditioned...surrounded by shops and facilities to meet every requirement of the guest.' Such was indeed the case with shops and businesses of every sort surrounding the lobby and based within the hotel, although full air conditioning of the hotel wasn't completed in 1952.

**Frank Schutt,** the 1925 Peabody's 1st manager.

It was at this point that the Peabody undertook measures that would ultimately result in its international status, this, largely, due to the executive abilities of project head Albert Parker. The preparations for the hotel's construction, staffing, and operation were overseen by Parker, with especial attention to detail. He hired Frank Schutt, who had served as assistant manager of the Biltmore Hotel in Atlanta, as the new Peabody's first manager. There was no way Parker could have foreseen at the time how significant the hiring of Frank Schutt as the new Peabody Hotel's manager would ultimately prove to be to the Peabody's history. In retrospect, it seems to have been one of those rare, almost providential decisions. But Schutt was well qualified for the job, not only personally, but almost genetically. Schutt's great-grandfather had opened a chain of taverns in New York. Schutt's grandfather, J.L.Schutt built and opened the Laurel House in 1801, the first resort hotel in the Catskills. Schutt's mother's side of the family opened the Catskill Mountain House in 1805. Schutt's father, L.P.Schutt was manager of the Casa Marina in Key West and associated with the Flagler companies for thirty years. Both of his brothers were also involved in hotel management. Schutt would eventually be responsible for not only the famous Peabody ducks, but The Skyway, two decisions which still resonate today.

The vision for the new Peabody Hotel was that it should offer both elegance and comfort. To that end, all staff members were carefully chosen and trained in the nuances of personal service. As the construction continued, the magnificent one piece carved marble fountain, which would later hold the famous ducks, was placed in the center of the hotel's ornate lobby, and $500,000 in furniture, a very large sum for 1925, was placed throughout the hotel. Intricately carved wood and plaster were installed on the walls and ceiling of both lobby and mezzanine. In short, everything possible was done to assure that the Peabody would not only be the grandest hotel in Memphis, but in the entire South.

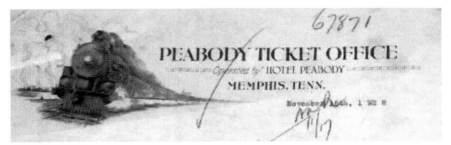

Total L & N Railroad ticket sales at the Peabody Ticket Office in the month of October, 1928, were $65,407.50 from 5,236 tickets, according to A.L Parker, the Peabody's ticket agent at the time.

**The elegant lobby** of the new hotel soon became a gathering place for the city's and ultimately many of the nation's elite.

With preparations completed, the hotel was set to officially open at 6:00 a.m. on the morning of September 2, 1925. But on the previous evening, September 1, a fabulous preview party was held for a private guest list consisting of 1,200 notables. The invitation to this gala event featured a picture of the new Hotel Peabody as it was then known under which were printed the words 'The South's Finest-One of America's Best.' This appealing slogan stuck and remained in force for many decades.

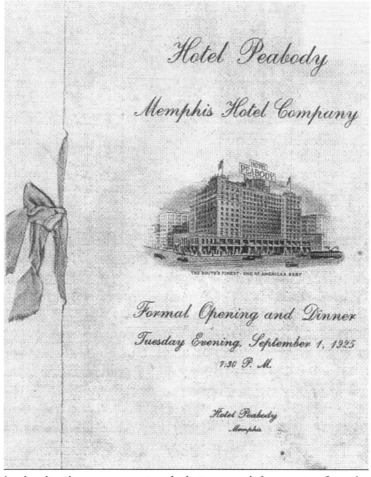

**This invitation** was extended to special guests for the grand opening of the new $5 million hotel. The opening festivities offered a dedication, a seated dinner with speech, and dancing in the ball room. Those in attendance at this gala preview party were treated to a magnificent dinner and a night of dancing, live music and revelry. The hotel's staff of 450 worked through the night and were ready and still on duty when the hotel officially opened the next morning as scheduled.

**The Peabody Bell Staff** posed for this photo near the hotel's entrance.

On September 2, 1925 the Memphis *Commercial Appeal* printed the following article welcoming the new Peabody:

## "GREAT DAY FOR PEABODY; GREAT DAY FOR MEMPHIS

This morning the Peabody Hotel, having more than 600 rooms, is open for business. It is as fine as any hotel in the United States. Architecturally it is a challenge to the creative imagination of the lovers of the beautiful. Its interior appointments and furnishings are rich and elegant. There is a note of refinement and taste from the ground floor to the skylight.

The readers of the *Commercial Appeal* may gather some idea of what this hotel is when they are told that more than 5,000 cars were used in bringing for the work of construction and completion, material from all corners of the earth. In ground area the Peabody is the largest in the South. It is larger in earth coverage than any hotel in New York City.

Already the Peabody has brought into its being some of the fine old traditions of Memphis inn keeping. The old Peabody bore no mean part in the history of Memphis. In days that were dark in the long ago when Death turned his machine guns on Memphis the old Peabody remained open and served the well and the sick.

And in the old Peabody many things were talked about and acted upon which resulted in the development of the City of Memphis.

Intimately associated with the old Peabody was an old Memphis family. Associated with the new Peabody is the same Memphis family-the Snowdens. Latterly the Parkers had much to do with the hotels in Memphis. They are builders, these Parkers. They were largely instrumental in the rebuilding of the old Gayoso. They had to with the construction of the Gayoso and Chisca, and one of them, A.L. Parker, was with the new Peabody from the making of the first blueprint until the formal opening last night.

The new Peabody Hotel cost more than $5,000,000. This sum is large, but this is an era of big things, and big things demand big money.

The Peabody should earn and will earn a handsome return on the investment. It is more than a hotel. It is an institution. It brings added value to Memphis. It adds values to adjacent property. But more than this, the Peabody can comfortably house and entertain people from any part of the United States in a manner equal to the service offered by the best hotels in America.

The Peabody is a tremendous asset to Memphis. It is in mortar and stone an expression of the faith that Memphians and men who are not Memphians have in this city. It is another evidence that

Memphis is a place where strangers may come and invest their money and be assured of fair and decent treatment by our citizens and by those officials who have the affairs of our city in charge.

When the old Peabody was started The *Appeal* was just licking its sores following the Civil War. There was always a spirit of good feeling between this paper and The Peabody. Proprietors and attaches in the past were always courteous to our representatives. The new Peabody is just down the street from us. It is an old friend and an old neighbor dressed up in modern clothing.

We are sure that it will succeed. We know it will serve its patrons and friends in that spirit of unostentatious kindness and hospitality which brings from the recipient an affectionate regard.

This is a big day for The Peabody, but it is a bigger day for Memphis. It is also a big day for The *Commercial Appeal*, because we love to see old friends and neighbors prosper and accomplish successfully those things they set out to do.

The proprietors of The Peabody set out to build as fine a hotel as there is in the nation. They have succeeded.

N.B.-In the new Peabody Messrs. Newman and Saunders of New Orleans are moving spirits. This, then is just another evidence of the faith of these sterling men in Memphis and its people."

**The elevator lobby** was uncluttered and elegant.

**Main elevators alternate view**

Those familiar with older hotels in major cities will remember that it was once common practice for merchants of all types to have offices and shops in hotels, usually on the mezzanine and main levels, with some even located below the main floor. This tradition, abandoned largely in the 1960s as the result of suburban expansion, has again come into vogue as many downtown areas nationwide are once again thriving. Between the 1920s and 1960s the Peabody featured more than 40 shops and offices of various types positioned around the lobby and mezzanine areas, although all of the original business spaces were not fully occupied until 1934.

A CHRONICLE OF WEEKLY SOCIAL AND BUSINESS ACTIVITIES OF WHICH

HOTEL PEABODY

Hotel Peabody

**Cover of *Hi-Lites*** During the late 1920s, and possibly beyond, the hotel published its own weekly in house magazine, `Hi-Lites' which detailed upcoming events at the hotel, provided information of local interest to guests such as theatre and train schedules, a hotel directory, and featured advertisements from some of the merchants located at The Peabody. In this era, most everything was downtown, including theatres, restaurants, car dealerships, libraries, hotels, department stores, etc. The train and bus stations brought people from all over the country to large cities. Like other major downtown areas, The Peabody benefitted from the easy access provided by railroads.

# HOTEL DIRECTORY

Accountants—Oliver P. Cobb & Co., Mezzanine Floor.

Air Service—"Mid-South Airways, Inc." East Lobby, Third Street Entrance.

Art and Decorative Objects —Luxemburg's East Lobby Entrance.

Automobiles for Hire—Taxi Stand.

Book Shop— "Three Musketeers, Inc." East Lobby, Third Street.

Beauty Parlor—Peabody Marinello Shop. Expert Service. Mezzanine Floor.

Barber Shop—Grill room foyer.

Bostonian Shoes, also furnishings for men, Hotel Lobby.

Check Room—Hats, umbrellas, grips, etc. Ask bell boy to direct you.

Cigar Stand—Right in Main Lobby at elevators.

Drive Ur Self Cabs—Taxi Stand.

Drug Store—The Peabody, west, Main Lobby.

Dentists—Mezzanine Floor, Room 208. Phone for appointment.

Florists—Off Main Lobby. Irby Harris.

Fur Shoppe—Main Lobby.

Identification Service—Waggener Finger Print Corporation. 94 South Second St.

Laundry—Call laundry boy.

Lending Library—"Three Musketeers, Inc." Lobby at Third Street Entrance.

Local and Long Distance Phones—Southeast corner, Main Lobby.

Maitre d'Hotel—Lobby floor, east.

Motor Cars—Hudson and Essex. Third St. entrance. Memphis Motor Car Co.

Main Restaurant—A la Carte service for all meals. Special club breakfast, table d'hote dinner and lunch. Off Main Lobby, east entrance.

Notary Public—Mezzanine Floor, Room 205.

Newsstand—In front of Main Lobby.

Osteopathic Physician—Mezzanine Floor Room 206.

Picture Framing—Kodaks, films, cards. Memphis Photo Supply Co., Second St. Entrance.

Peabody Gown Shoppe—Women's dresses, coats, hats, accessories. Off Main Lobby. Anette K. Robinson.

Photographer—207.

Public Stenographer—Correspondence, legal, technical, tabulations, copying, etc. Men's writing room, off Main Lobby.

Poodle Dog Grill—6 a.m. to 12 p.m. Basement.

Peabody Catering Co.—Third Street entrance. Mrs. Frayser in charge.

Postal Telegraph—Off Main Lobby.

Patterson Transfer Co.—Off Main Lobby, north entrance.

Room Service—For all services to rooms.

Railroad Office—Tickets and reservations to all parts of the world. Main Lobby.

Sports Shop—Sporting goods of character. Off Main Lobby, Second St. entrance.

The Rose Shop, Millinery—Third Street and Union, East Lobby entrance.

Tea Room—East off Main Lobby. All kinds of sodas, ices, parfaits, teas, etc.

Valet—Day and night service. Call L. S. Loyd.

Yellow Cab Service—Southwest entrance.

## Hotel Directory

The Peabody was basically a city within itself, offering services of all kinds. A look at the hotel directory quickly illustrates the full range of options available to hotel guests. There was a camera shop, news stand, car rental agency, cigar stand, fur shop, a Hudson and Essex car dealership, taxi stand, drug store, shoe store, airline and train ticket office, beauty parlor, dentist, osteopath, sports shop, notary public, accountant, florist, lending library, laundry, and local and long distance telephone office.

**TRAINS ARRIVING AT AND DEPARTING FROM GRAND CENTRAL STATION**
Corner Main St. and Calhoun Ave., Memphis, Tennessee
Ticket Office operated by Hotel Peabody in Hotel Lobby       J. G. McKinnon, *Manager*
Corrected to February 26, 1928—Central Standard Time

## ILLINOIS CENTRAL

| Train No. | ARRIVES | Train No. | DEPARTS |
|---|---|---|---|
| 7 Panama Limited | 12:31 a.m. | 7 Panama Limited | 12:36 a.m. |
| 2 From New Orleans, Jackson | 6:35 a.m. | 2 For Chicago, St. Louis &- | |
| 15 The Chickasaw | 7:30 a.m. | Louisville | 6:50 a.m. |
| 3 From Chicago | 8:15 a.m. | 126 Fulton Local | 7:50 a.m. |
| 103 From Cincinnati, Louisville, | | 133 Grenada Local | 8:15 a.m. |
| St. Louis | 8:20 a.m. | 3 For Jackson & New Orleans | 9:10 a.m. |
| 132 Grenada Local | 9:00 a.m. | 110 For Chicago, St Louis | 4:35 p.m. |
| 133 Fulton Local | 9:10 a.m. | 131 Grenada Local | 5:00 p.m. |
| 134 Grenada Local | 4:30 p.m. | 4 For Chicago | 7:35 p.m. |
| 125 Fulton Local | 6:40 p.m. | 104 For Louisville & Cincinnati | 9:10 p.m. |
| 4 From New Orleans, Jackson | 6:55 p.m. | 8 For St. Louis & Chicago | |
| 8 From New Orleans | 9:00 p.m. | (Sleeping car only) | 9:05 p.m. |
| 1 From Chicago, St. Louis and | | 16 The Chickasaw | 11:20 p.m. |
| Louisville | 11:25 p.m. | 1 For Jackson, New Orleans | 11:50 p.m. |

## FRISCO LINES

| | | | |
|---|---|---|---|
| 805 Memphian | 7:05 a.m. | 921 Birmingham Local | 7:10 a.m. |
| 108 Sunnyland | 7:20 a.m. | 108 Sunnyland to Kansas City | 7:45 a.m. |
| 105 Kansas City-Florida Special | 7:45 a.m. | 808 Sunnyland to St. Louis | 8:00 a.m. |
| 924 From Mobile and Aberdeen | 8:30 a.m. | 105 Kansas City-Florida Special | 8:05 a.m. |
| 922 Birmingham Local | 5:50 p.m. | 802 St. Louis Express | 9:00 a.m. |
| 103 Kansas City Express | 6:55 p.m. | 104 Kansas City Express | 9:15 a.m. |
| 801 St. Louis Express | 6:55 p.m. | 923 For Aberdeen and Mobile | 5:30 p.m. |
| 106 Kansas City-Florida Special | 7:20 p.m. | 106 Kansas City-Florida Special | 7:45 p.m. |
| 807 Sunnyland from St. Louis | 8:45 p.m. | 107 Sunnyland | 9:35 p.m. |
| 107 Sunnyland from Colorado & | | 806 Memphian | 11:20 p.m. |
| Kansas City | 9:15 p.m. | | |

## CHICAGO, ROCK ISLAND & PACIFIC RAILROAD

| | | | |
|---|---|---|---|
| 112 Memphis-Californian | 6:40 a.m. | 49 Hot Springs-Panama Limited | 12:45 a.m. |
| 42 Choctaw Limited | 12:45 p.m. | 603 Little Rock Passenger | 7:00 a.m. |
| 604 Passenger | 4:55 p.m. | 45 Hot Springs Limited | 8:30 a.m. |
| 46 Hot Springs Limited | 6:55 p.m. | 41 Choctaw Limited | 2:30 p.m. |
| 50 Hot Springs-Panama Limited | 9:00 p.m. | 111 Californian | 9:05 p.m. |

## YAZOO & MISSISSIPPI VALLEY RAILROAD

| | | | |
|---|---|---|---|
| 12 Northern Express | 6:25 a.m. | 21 Traveler's Special | 1:15 a.m. |
| 32 Tutwiler & Lambert | 10:20 a.m. | 23 Delta Express | 8:40 a.m. |
| 30 G'ville, G'wood, Clarkdale | 10:30 a.m. | 31 Yazoo City-Tutwiler | 9:05 a.m. |
| 24 Vicksburg & Clarkdale | 4:10 p.m. | 33 Lambert & Tutwiler | 3:30 p.m. |
| 34 Yazoo City-Tutwiler | 4:25 p.m. | 39 C'dale, Tutwiler, G'wood | 4:00 p.m. |
| 26 C'land, G'ville & Clarkdale | 7:00 p.m. | 15 Southern Express | 5:00 p.m. |

All Trains run daily, including Sunday, unless otherwise specified
Note changes in Illinois Central Trains

## Grand Central Station train schedule

Like most major cities of the era, Memphis was a significant railroad center. This 1928 schedule of arriving and departing trains from Grand Central Station provides an example. It was literally possible to reach nearly any place in America by rail, through connecting trains. Many of the trains had names like the `Panama Limited,' the `Florida Special', `Hummingbird,' and `South Wind.' As with modern airports, where there are multiple terminals serving different airlines, there was more than one train station in Memphis. Union Station was the place for L. & N., Missouri Pacific, Southern, Cotton Belt, and N.C. & St. L. Train schedules for both stations were always published in `Hi-Lites.'

63

**Memphis was also served by Union Station.**

One of the many businesses operating within the Peabody was the Peabody's own Peabody Steamship and Tourist Agency. This agency opened at the same time as the hotel in 1925 and conducted tours and made detailed travel arrangements. A newspaper article from the 1930s described its services as follows:

`No matter what ship the traveler desires to make his crossing on, no matter what Parisian cafe he wishes to visit for a carefree half-hour, no matter what size camel he wants for his pilgrimage to the Pyramids, the Hotel Peabody Steamship and Tourist Agency has the arrangements within its scope. The traveler who leaves his itinerary and comfort in their hands has no worries.'

During the 1930s, the Peabody also had its Peabody Catering Company which made custom ordered wedding cakes and other pastries which were famous throughout the nation. In addition to these businesses, there were open ballrooms which were rented for conventions, weddings, private parties, and other events, a tradition which continues in the hotel to the present day.

**A friendly staff always awaited guests at the registration desk.**

Every large hotel offered a barbershop, and the Peabody's was the finest available. Note the manicure table at the far end of the room and the sinks behind every chair. The large cast iron ceiling fans were functional rather than ornamental in the days before modern air conditioning.

**The women's beauty shop also featured manicure tables.**

Despite the opening of and competition from other significant hotels of the period, notably the Claridge, Parkview, King Cotton, Tennessee, the Peabody almost immediately established itself as Memphis' and the Mid-South's premier hotel, a title it still retains. Several elements have combined along with the passage of time, to earn The Peabody this unique reputation. First and foremost was the hotel's dedication to the comfort of its guests. Staff members prided themselves on remembering the names of the hotel's many patrons. This attention to detail only added to its reputation for the best in both food and service. One example involves the hotel's gift packs. A *Press Scimitar* article from 1952 mentioned that guests with advance reservations at the hotel found in their rooms small packages with their names printed in gold. Inside the packages were complimentary items tailored for either a woman or man guest, or both. Items included deodorant, shaving cream, hair tonic, lipstick, toothpaste, shampoo, and other items. Today most hotels and motels provide shampoo and hair conditioner, or skin lotion, but this was rare in the early 1950s, and the Peabody was one of the only hotels in North America to provide this service.

**The soda shop** offered a variety of cigars, toiletry items, coffee, and a soda fountain with milk shakes and ice cream.

## All Milk, Cream, Butter and Garden Products used at the Hotel are from our

# GAYOSO FARMS

### HORN LAKE, MISSISSIPPI

The Gayoso Farms of 684 Acres, located at Horn Lake, Mississippi, fourteen miles south of Hotel Peabody on the Memphis-Hernando Road, are owned and operated by the Memphis Hotel Company for the purpose of furnishing its hotels in Memphis (The Peabody, Gayoso and Chisca) with "Golden Yellow" Guernsey Milk and Cream, "Leading in Quality" Hampshire meat and orchard and garden products—indicative of the high standard of service it has established and maintains.

For years a definite breeding program has been carried on in both the Guernsey and Hampshire Departments. Through careful selection, skillful mating—using best sires, and proper care and feeding, both the herds have been developed to first rank in their respective breeds in the South, and among the first in the United States.

*Gayoso's Roberta's Actor*

This advertisement from *Hi-Lites* promoting Gayoso Farms was intended to inform hotel guests that the meat and dairy products served in the Peabody as well as in The Gayoso, and Chisca hotels, were of the highest quality obtainable, as indeed they were. The Peabody Hotel opened under the umbrella of the Memphis Hotel Company, which, at the time, owned all three of Memphis' most important downtown hotels.

**The ladies' shop** sold purses, handbags, linens, and jewelry in addition to dresses.

**Lloyd's Liquor Store** was located in The Peabody.

**The Billiard Room** shown here was probably located in the basement.

**A 1925 corner room**. Note the large steam powered radiator which provided heat in the winter months. The windows were functional and provided both ventilation and cooling in the summer.

**A larger corner suite.**

**1925 era guest room**. In the early days of large downtown hotels, rooms weren't very big, even in large hotels. When Jack Belz restored The Peabody a decision had been made to reduce the number of rooms from the original 625 to approximately 400, thus creating fewer, but larger rooms in keeping with the desires of modern guests who expected larger, more comfortable rooms, especially in luxury hotels.

But what really made the Peabody famous in terms of entertainment were its concerts on the roof. Hotel roof top concerts were not uncommon during the pre-World War II era at large hotels in places like Miami, and other large, often Southern cities. Even Memphis had rooftop dances and concerts at the Magnolia Roof Gardens at the Hotel Claridge. And yet, it was the roof top concerts and dances at the Peabody which became famous. This tradition started as early as 1926, less than a year after the new hotel opened. The first outdoor roof garden was called the Owl's Nest. An article in the *Commercial Appeal* described the opening evening's festivities:

`All of Society turned out last night for the first try at the new roof garden, the Owl's Nest, which lies atop Hotel Peabody. Under the light of the big full moon, some 500 of the city's elite gathered to spend a delightful evening dining, dancing and enjoying a program of cabaret numbers. The spacious roof of the hotel has been transformed into an outdoor garden, with iron tables, striped awnings and two large dance floors. The Seven Aces orchestra provided music for as many as cared to Charleston or waltz in the cool breeze. Judging from the opening night of the garden, it will be the gathering place of society during the long summer months.'

This open part of the roof served as a dance area before later being enclosed as 'The Skyway.'

**Benny Goodman**          **The Andrews Sisters**

**Harry James**         **Glenn Miller**

**Ted Weems**                    **Jan Garber**

## Nite Cap Club

Another grand tradition began with the opening of the new Peabody Hotel, the tradition of the Peabody Hotel as the premier location for some of the best live music in the nation. Within a year of opening, the new hotel had Friday night dining and dancing in a private club called the Nite Cap Club which was started by a group of locals in the hotel's former Italian Room. Nationally prominent orchestras of the era regularly played various locations at the

Peabody. This was the big band era and the musicians and performers were literally the top recording and touring acts in America. Among the favorites were George Hamilton, Blue Steele, Oswald Lobrecue, Carlos Molina, Jan Garber, Paul Whiteman, Ray Anthony, Ted Weems, Les Brown, Benny Goodman, Harry James, Lawrence Welk, Ozzie Nelson, Dorothy Lamour, Snooky Lanson, the Andrews Sisters, Glenn Miller, and other top names too numerous to mention.

**Snooky Lanson**            **Paul Whiteman**

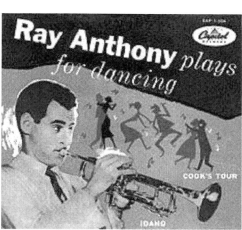

**Les Brown**            **Ray Anthony**

Whether it was in the hotel lobby, one of the large rooms like the Continental Ballroom, or concerts for dancing on the roof under the stars, the Peabody was the place to be. For a time, in fact, beginning in 1937, CBS radio broadcast local WREC radio's concerts live on the radio from the roof. There is nothing like being on the roof of The Peabody on a warm summer night.

The Peabody was a prestigious venue for many touring bands, and popular musicians who played there, often sent mailers announcing their upcoming appearance. A good size crowd helped considerably to assure a repeat engagement, as was the case with this mailer from entertainer Chuck Cabot.

Over the early years the name of The Peabody's roof changed several times. It was alternately called the Moroccan Roof, the Marine Roof, and finally, in 1938, became known as The Plantation Roof, a name which was due to the construction of a Southern mansion facade on top of the roof, a structure which remains to this day. The Plantation Roof was originally intended to be named the `Tara Roof' after Scarlett O'Hara's house in `Gone With the Wind,' but the name `Plantation Roof' had the same connotation without any potential legal entanglements.

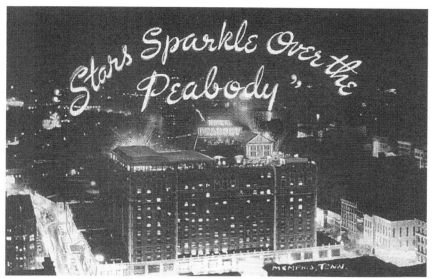

**`Stars Sparkle Over the Peabody'**

The Plantation Roof on a summer night. It doesn't get any better, and it is the perfect place for an open air wedding reception, convention, birthday celebration, or any other festive occasion. The Peabody's courteous and efficient staff can make any event the memory of a lifetime.

While standing on the roof and watching barges move slowly toward New Orleans on a sultry summer night, it's difficult to imagine it could ever be otherwise, but Memphis does get cold in the winter. The popularity of the profitable rooftop concerts needed to be extended beyond the warmer weather. In 1938, Frank Schutt, the same hotel manager responsible for the Peabody ducks, was given approval by the hotel's board of directors to create a covered circular ballroom on the top floor of the hotel. Architects George Mahan and Nowland Van Powell were selected as designers, and Fred Young and Sam Maury were selected as general contractors. The project was formally announced in October, 1938. This new, round facility would feature removable floor to ceiling windows, as well as raised seating similar to that found in major Las Vegas showrooms. Popular rooftop dancing would be improved with a new 2000 sq. ft. circular beechwood dance floor with a 64 ft. diameter. It was felt that a unique facility of this type would allow the hotel to provide big name entertainment year round. Additionally, the new room would be an excellent location for large social events of all types, having nearly twice the capacity of the downstairs ballroom, and providing even more revenues for the hotel.

Manager Frank Schutt, the most significant manager in the hotel's early history, was responsible for the Skyway and ducks.

**The New Skyway was perfect in design and execution.**

The plan was approved and the construction undertaken with a final cost expected to be in excess of $100,000. Several names had been suggested, including the Regency Room, Aurora Terrace, the Rainbow Room, and Garden of the Moon, although at the time of the announcement no name had been chosen. It was, despite its modernistic `swank' design, a major construction project. Over 90 tons of steel had to be transported to the top of the hotel through temporary outside elevators. When the project was completed a grand opening celebration was held January 1, 1939, and 1,200 revelers attended the opening festivities, tickets for which were sold out weeks in advance.

Henry King and his orchestra provided the entertainment and a magnificent lobster feast was served at midnight. The new showroom situated on top of the hotel was aptly named the `Skyway' and was the equal of any in the nation. The domed circular ceiling was painted midnight blue and punctuated with recessed lights, giving the impression of being under a night sky. While the new room occupied a substantial part of the roof area formerly used for concerts and dancing, more than enough of the original area still remained for parties and dancing in an outside area on the roof. The new enclosed rooftop facility was an immediate success, and remains so today, nearly eighty years later.

**Henry King and his Orchestra opened the new Skyway**

Like the Plantation Roof, the Skyway may be configured as desired for dining, dancing, or both. Its design is truly timeless, and the Skyway remains as popular as it was when first opened.

**Skyway Menu Cover** `Atop Hotel Peabody. The famous hotel had been called the Peabody Hotel when it opened in 1869. By the time the 2nd hotel opened in 1925, it was officially called Hotel Peabody. Today, it is technically The Peabody, but is still referred to by its other names as well. No matter what it is called, everybody anywhere, knows exactly what you mean.

**Peabody matches were offered free at the Peabody.**

**Fresh Gulf Shrimp,**
**Remoulade** .......... 1.00
with a famous sauce made of
creole mustard and horseradish
or cocktail sauce.

**Onion Soup au Gratin** ..... 50
made from an old French
recipe topped with cheese
and croutons.

**Chilled Tomato Bouillon** ... 30

**Fresh Orange Juice** ......... 50

**Lump Crabmeat**
**Ravigotte** .......... 1.00
served with a creamy white
sauce made with pimentos,
green pepper, English mustard.

**Fresh Assorted Fruit**
**Cocktail Supreme** ....... 70

**Split Pea Soup, Croutons** .. 35

**Assorted Canapes** ......... 75

**Chilled Tomato Juice** ..... 30

**Old-Fashioned Vegetable**
**Soup** .......... 40

**Fresh Cream of Tomato**
**Soup** .......... 40

**Stuffed Celery with**
**Blue Cheese** .......... 85

---

## ENTREES

**Flaming Shishkabob** .......... 3.50
chunks of choice tenderloin, slices of tomato,
onion and pepper, fresh mushrooms broiled
on a sword and served aflame. French fries.

**Filet Mignon** .......... 4.50
an 8 ounce aged cut of tenderloin served
with fresh mushrooms. French fries.

**French Cut Double Lamb Chops Mirabeau** 4.25
with the zest of charcoal flavor. Served with
tomato and mint jelly.

**Chateaubriand (1 lb.), Garni with**
**Bearnaise Sauce** .......... 9.00
a juicy cut of beef tenderloin, aged and good,
prepared by Chef Mason. Served with fresh
vegetables this is a real treat for two.

**U. S. Choice 12 Ounce Sirloin Steak,**
**Maitre d'Hotel** .......... 5.25
a great cut of beef, charcoal smoked. Served
with potato, butter and fresh watercress.

**Rock Cornish Game Hen** .......... 3.25
the delicate flavor of this game and the tender
white meat accompanied by pecan dressing and
orange sauce would please a King.
(30-45 minutes.)

**Grilled Sugar-Cured Ham Steak** .......... 2.75
broiled Pineapple and French fried potatoes.

**Roast Prime Ribs of Beef au jus** .......... 3.65
cooked the English way with heavy salt and
served with a giant baked potato with sour cream,
chives and bacon chips. Tossed dinner salad.

**Lobster Thermidor** .......... 4.50
fresh from Maine, the tender meat of this lobster
is blended with fresh mushrooms to make
this a true Memphis treat. Julienne potatoes.

**Fried Half Spring Chicken** .......... 2.25
fried the Southern way and served with a
spiced peach, honey and corn fritters.

**Chopped Beef Tenderloin Tips** .......... 2.25
juicy tenderloin tips, ground, then cooked to your
desire and served with stuffed onion.

**Broiled Fresh Brook Trout (2)** .......... 3.50
with almandine butter and tartare sauce.
Baked potato or French fries.

**Peabody Jr. Special 6 oz. Sirloin** .......... 3.50
charcoal broiled to your order with
baked or French fried potatoes.

**Fried Louisiana Jumbo Shrimp** .......... 2.85
Served with Julienne potatoes, fried onion rings
and Tartare sauce.

**Breaded Veal Cutlet** .......... 2.50
spaghetti milanaise.

——— THE ABOVE ENTREES INCLUDE ROLLS AND BUTTER, COFFEE OR TEA ———

**Fresh Vegetables may be substituted for Potatoes on above orders**

DINNER GUESTS REMAINING AFTER 5 P.M. ARE SUBJECT TO 20% FEDERAL TAX ON ALL ITEMS
Guests Served Dinner Before 5 P.M. May Remain for Dancing, Except Friday and Saturday Without Cover Charge

**We Will Be Pleased to Serve You Any Items Not Listed at a la Carte Prices.**

## BEVERAGES

**Cafe, pot** .......... 30    **Tea, hot or chilled** .......... 25    **Milk or Buttermilk** .......... 25

## Skyway Menu

These two menu pages give some indication of the type and variety
of food items available, and are indicative of how The Peabody
developed such a great reputation for wonderful food. Despite the
high cost of the Skyway's construction, it proved to have been a
wise investment.

## SALADES

| | |
|---|---|
| Peabody Fruit Plate.............1.75 | Chef's Cotton King Salad Bowl.........1.50 |
| created especially for the Skyway Room — a Summertime surprise. | lettuce, romaine, watercress tossed together and topped with chopped eggs, julienne of ham and turkey, anchovy, oil and vinegar. |
| Watercress Salad...............65 | |
| with chopped hard boiled eggs and a tangy Blue Cheese dressing. | Head Lettuce...................35 |
| | with 1000 Island or French dressing. Blue Cheese dressing 25c extra. |
| Louisiana Shrimp Salad Plate..........1.50 | |
| | Crisp Tossed Dinner Salad..........35 |
| Hearts of Lettuce and Tomato........50 | with 1000 Island or French dressing. Blue Cheese dressing 25c extra. |
| your favorite dressing, bacon chips. | |

## A LA CARTE

| | | LEGUMES | |
|---|---|---|---|
| Cheese or Mushroom Omelette.........1.25 | | Stuffed Onions.................35 | |
| Eggs Benedict..................1.50 | | French Fried Potatoes............30 | |
| boiled ham and poached eggs on crisp toast. Hollandaise sauce. | | Asparagus Spears, Butter..........60 | |
| Peabody Club Sandwich...........1.25 | | String Beans Almandine............35 | |
| slices of turkey, crisp bacon, lettuce and tomato served with potato chips. | | Fresh Corn on the Cob............35 | |
| Grilled Ham Steak.............2.25 | | Broccoli au Beurre..............35 | |
| with eggs. | | Potatoes au Gratin.............40 | |
| Turkey and Ham au Gratin.........2.00 | | Baked Potato.................40 | |
| with julienne potatoes. | | filled with butter, chives and bacon. | |

## DESSERTS

| | |
|---|---|
| Crepes Suzette................1.00 | Peach Melba...................50 |
| prepared at your table and set aflame. | created for the famous singer Melba by the great chef A. Escoffier. This dessert has been a gourmet's delight for years. A whole peach stuffed with ice cream topped with the famous Melba sauce and sprinkled with toasted almonds. |
| Strawberry Romanoff............1.00 | |
| Skyway Ice Box Pies............35 | |
| blackbottom, coconut and lemon. Graham cracker crust. | |
| Fruit Sherbets................35 | Alaska Flambe.................75 |
| Creme de Menthe, Strawberry or | Ice Cream....................20 |
| Chocolate Parfait.............40 | Vanilla, Chocolate or Strawberry served with Petits Fours. |
| Coupe de St. Jacques...........60 | |
| when Brother John was sleeping he dreamed of this dessert: a macedoine of six fresh fruits marinated in fine brandy, topped with three scoops of assorted ices. | Eclair Eugene.................1.00 |
| | the shell is filled with vanilla ice cream and covered with a fabulous sauce made at your table —chocolate, creme de cacao and fine brandy. |
| Charlotte Russe..............40 | Cherries Jubilee...............1.00 |
| Bavarian Cream au Sherry, decorated with lady fingers and topped with whipped cream. | ice cream and black bing cherries flamed at your table. |

———— ALL ITEMS SERVED UNTIL HALF PAST MIDNIGHT ————

**Another Peabody matchbook cover.** It successfully advertised dining, dancing, big name orchestras, and the hotel coffee shop in a rather small area.

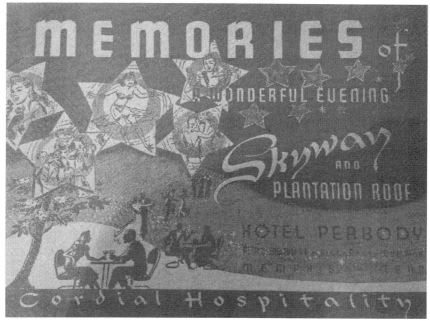

**A cover for a souvenir photo**. In much of The Peabody's recent advertising a lot has been said about making memories. It is certainly no exaggeration. Everyone who visits, has a drink in the lobby, watches the ducks, attends a dance on the roof, a party, wedding reception, convention, or just spends the night, takes along with them a feeling almost of nostalgia. It's difficult to explain but easily understood.

Joe Sudduth, the Peabody's in house photographer for nearly sixty years, was always on hand to capture special moments for the Skyway and Plantation Roof's many patrons. In the early days his photographs were taken with a Graflex press camera which used individual film plates for each photograph. When processed, the photographs arrived within a cover like the one seen here. Several exterior colors were available but the cover art itself remained unchanged. Photographs were available in both 8"x 10" and 5"x 7" sizes. During his tenure at the hotel, he recorded thousands of memories for guests and patrons which returned home with them to literally all parts of the globe.

**`The Skyway Atop Hotel Peabody-Memphis, Tennessee'** This somewhat imaginative Skyway menu cover manages to accurately convey the spirit of a night of dancing at the Skyway. The Skyway immediately became the favorite spot in Memphis for large meetings and luncheons, as well as for indoor dancing and dining.

These World War II era photographs of people enjoying the Skyway came from the Peabody's Memorabilia Room on the Mezzanine level. They are just a small sampling of the photographs on hand. Additionally there are letters, menus, china, silverware, glasses, postcards, and other souvenirs of the hotel's long history. A recorded message leads the visitor through the interesting history of the hotel.

Drinks on the Skyway or Plantation Roof, are a Memphis tradition.

The future Mr. and Mrs. Jack Belz. Marilyn Belz, third from left, and Jack Belz, third from right, second row. It's doubtful that when this picture was made that Jack Belz had even the slightest idea that he would someday rescue the landmark hotel and become such a significant part of The Peabody's history.

SOUTHERN AIR SERVICE, INC.

REQUESTS YOUR PRESENCE

AT

DAWN PATROL BANQUET AND DANCE

GEORGIAN ROOM

HOTEL PEABODY

MONDAY EVENING, DECEMBER TWENTIETH

NINETEEN HUNDRED AND THIRTY-SEVEN

7 P.M.

INFORMAL                    GUEST RESERVATION
R. S. V. P.                     ON REQUEST

A 1933 invitation from Southern Air Service is typical of the hotel's prewar activities. An earlier, 1933 invitation to a `Special

Concert Dinner' looked like great fun. The menu was inviting and so was the entertainment, trombonist Glenn Miller, who would eventually become the most successful and popular bandleader of his time. Many famous people as well as those who would later become so played The Peabody regularly.

Movie star Dorothy Lamour basically got her start at the Peabody. While in a talent contest she was spotted by Peabody band leader Herbie Kay who happened to be in the audience. Introduced as the `Miss New Orleans of 1931,' the young singer impressed bandleader Kay, who soon hired her to sing with The Peabody Orchestra at the Skyway. Kay and Lamour were subsequently married from 1935 to 1939. From the Peabody, Lamour went on to sing with Rudy Vallee, and became the first vocalist to sing at New York City's famed Stork Club. Her singing resulted in her development into an actress. She starred in the 1940 classic, `The Road to Singapore,' the first of the great Bob Hope and Bing Crosby `Road' films. Dorothy Lamour enjoyed a long and successful career in Hollywood and made almost fifty movies.

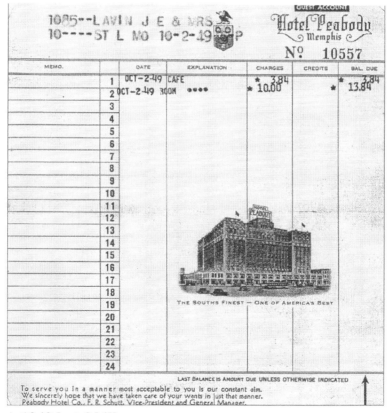

**A 1949 hotel bill**

**Chuck Foster**

Singer Chuck Foster's liner notes from the back of his `Chuck Foster at Hotel Peabody...' evoked the spirit of the Peabody:

"The muddy Mississippi winds its way to the gulf, lazily flowing by Memphis, where towering bluffs look down. Year in and year out the bluffs see the barges carry away the cotton that provides the wherewithal for the good life that the Southern agriculturalist enjoys. Just outside of Memphis is the sprawling Delta country of Mississippi and Arkansas presided over by affluent planters who like to come up to Memphis for their holidays. The often repeated phrase attributed to William Faulkner-"The Delta begins in the lobby of the Hotel Peabody" is no exaggeration.

"The Peabody is something of an institution in these parts, and along with the Peabody one thinks of Chuck Foster. Playing his usual month's engagement around the Christmas and New Year's holidays, Chuck provides the musical background for the gaiety that goes along with the festive season which is also a time of honoring Delta debutantes. When June brings balmy days, when the cotton is planted and the Southern gentleman wants to relax and drink his bourbon and branch water, again he treks to Memphis and Hotel Peabody, and under the stars he dances to the music of Chuck Foster at the Skyway.

"Chuck Foster, also is an institution. Since 1943 he has played two lengthy engagements per year in Memphis. A veteran showman who got his start on the west coast prior to World War II, Chuck plays smooth arrangements that are danceable and listenable from the first strains of the theme. Chuck has played at distinguished hotels throughout the country and 'Music in the Foster Fashion' has provided the background for such glittering events as the Academy Awards Ball. Now you can make a ballroom of your own living room or patio, and join the fun loving people throughout the country who name Chuck Foster as their favorite bandleader."

The Officers, Directors and Members of the

**COTTON STATES FASHION EXHIBITORS**

INCORPORATED

Headquarters: 171 Monroe Avenue

Memphis, Tennessee

Invite You to Attend This

SPRING and SUMMER SHOWING

In Your Own Home Market

JANUARY 28 - 29 - 30, 1952

Monday - Tuesday - Wednesday

**AT THE PEABODY HOTEL**

Memphis, Tennessee

Yours For Better Service

**COTTON STATES FASHION EXHIBITORS**

The Cotton States Fashion Exhibitors headquarters were based in Memphis and its January, 1952 exhibition was held in its hometown at The Peabody. The meeting was supported by the Chamber of Commerce and the National Bureau of Salesmen. Now as then, there is no better place for a convention or meeting.

# THE COTTON CARNIVAL

The first Cotton Carnival, a three day long Mardi Gras type festival with an 'Old South' theme, took place in March, 1931, as part of a plan to raise the spirits of Memphians during the depression. It started an annual tradition which would continue through the early 1980s. As time passed, the Cotton Carnival became the most eagerly awaited Memphis social event of the year. The festival expanded from three days to a week, and due to weather conditions, moved from March to May. Krewes were organized for Cotton Carnival as with New Orleans' Mardi Gras. As time passed and the festival continued to grow, the Peabody Hotel served as a command center for much of this celebration of cotton, and an eagerly anticipated grand ball was held on the roof of the hotel every year. This May, 1954 invitation welcomes attendees to the opening of that year's Cotton Carnival. .

**The Cotton Carnival's letterhead was attractively designed.**

## THE SOUTH'S FINEST
## ONE OF AMERICA'S BEST

What is most impressive however, are the number of significant national publications in Memphis to cover the event. Cotton was king, and the Cotton Carnival was truly a big deal.

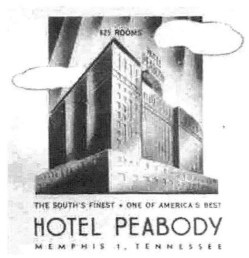

**Envelope image from 1949**. An air mail stamp was 6 cents.

**Peabody Kitchen 1949**

**Peabody Waitresses 1950s**

## The Problem of Souvenirs

Many people who consider themselves to be completely and totally honest seem to change character and fall into some sort of frenzy when they visit a hotel. They just want some sort of souvenir, a reminder of their pleasant stay. Nobody will miss one towel or an ashtray, or some other minor item, they reason. It seems that the more famous the hotel, the greater the problem. The removal of any items, no matter how seemingly insignificant, constitute an expense to any hotel. Multiply this by hundreds and sometimes thousands of times, and what seems at first glance minor, soon becomes an incredible expense. Theft from souvenir hunters, has always been a problem for the Peabody Hotel. In the past, guests regularly took towels, ashtrays, blankets, and basically anything else which depicted the hotel's distinctive logo, as souvenirs of their stay. At one time, as many as 6,000 pieces of silverware, 100 blankets, 350 bedspreads, 1,600 sheets, and nearly 11,000 towels, were taken yearly by visitors. Today, the public seems to be more conscious that removing hotel property ultimately results in higher room rates for everybody. And yet, in consideration of the Peabody's fame, it is understandable that any guest would want some sort of memento. For this reason, a wide variety of Peabody items of all types and in all price ranges are now always available at the shops in the hotel itself.

But hard times were on the horizon for the Memphis landmark. The Memphis Hotel Company, parent company of the Peabody, also owned the Gayoso, the Chisca, and other properties, most of which began losing money. In March, 1933, the Memphis Hotel Company went into receivership, and then into bankruptcy. The Peabody, while successful itself, had supplied money for the support of other unprofitable properties under the Memphis Hotel Company's umbrella. Money which should have contributed to the Peabody's maintenance and upkeep ended up elsewhere, and the quality of service as well as the physical condition of the building itself, consequently deteriorated.

**The 1925 Hotel Peabody** was intentionally self-contained. There was no reason to leave unless one had business outside its doors. A billiard room. Radio listening room, news and cigar stand, gym, beauty shop, and barber shop, as well as several restaurants were conveniently located within the hotel.

**Both the mezzanine and lobby have always offered comfortable seating for relaxing, reading, or socializing.**

Since the Peabody, on its own had always been profitable, even during the depression, it was removed from the list of other corporately owned properties and allowed to stand individually on its own merits under a reorganization known at the time, as the Peabody Hotel Company, Inc, which was owned by four families. The reorganized hotel continued to be managed by Frank Schutt, who also served as vice president. The president of the new operation was Henry Bunn, who had earlier been brought to Memphis from New Orleans to serve as president of the new Lowenstein's department store which had been built on the site of the first Peabody Hotel. Bunn had a long standing interest in the Peabody Hotel, and had, in fact, spent his wedding night at the first Peabody Hotel, thirty years earlier.

Under the reorganization, the hotel again prospered. The newly decorated Continental Ballroom opened on November 9, 1934 and constant parties, luncheons, conventions, and business meetings again became the order of the day. Crump Stadium opened nearby in 1934, and the Peabody Hotel became the hangout for Ole Miss and other football fans who came to town to see games at the new field. Through it all, the Peabody Hotel had survived and prospered. It made it through partial collapse, the yellow fever epidemic, reconstruction, relocation, the depression, competition from other hotels, receivership, bankruptcy, and reorganization. But soon, Memphians would turn elsewhere for a social gathering place due to the hotel's increased convention business. The constant presence of large numbers of out of towners eventually proved more than the locals could tolerate. Simply put, national conventions ran the locals off, even as the hotel's fame continued to grow throughout America.

The architectural attention to detail surrounding the entrance to one of the hotel's grand ballrooms is prevalent throughout every part of the Peabody.

The most famous quote ever spoken about The Peabody, and still related to this day, is taken from a 1935 book by David Lewis, entitled `God Shakes Creation.' In this book the following is written: "The Mississippi delta begins in the lobby of the Peabody Hotel and ends on Catfish Row in Vicksburg. The Peabody is the Paris Ritz, the Cairo Shepheards, the London Savoy of this section. If you stand near its fountain in the middle of the lobby, where ducks waddle, and turtles drowse, ultimately you will see everybody who is anybody in the delta." The same, identical quote is also attributed to David Cohn, 1935. The statement was well spoken and the point was well taken, regardless of who actually made the observation initially. Today, it is simply stated by Memphians that `The Delta begins in the lobby of the Peabody Hotel.'

Another, later quote from the *St. Louis Dispatch* of June, 1946, by reporter Rufas Terral said that "...Mississippians....are said to believe that when they die and go to heaven, it will be just like the Peabody lobby." These statements might seem a bit exaggerated today, and yet to those whose lives, and fortunes have paralleled those of the Peabody, as well as Memphis itself, such statements do not seem out of the ordinary at all. The Peabody Hotel, Memphis, the Mississippi River, and the people of the city are all interrelated in a finely woven and colorful tapestry.

### The Samovar
A November 8, 1935 newspaper article in the *Press Scimitar* proclaimed in large bold type `Exotic Atmosphere in Peabody's Samovar Room-Home of Nite Kap' In smaller headlines it stated `Elaborate Setting Will Vie With Parties There During Winter Season.' The text of the article

read:

"With the formal opening tonight of the Samovar room at Hotel Peabody, beginning the Nite Kap season, the new dance room will be filled with gay parties. The Samovar room itself will vie in interest with these parties. An authentic Russian samovar is placed in the modernistic orchestra stand as an insignia. Frank Schutt, manager of the Peabody found the samovar in an antique shop. After it had been polished, it was found to bear a Russian inscription. It is complete with charcoal burner, spigot, and stands two feet high. This antique was an inspiration for a name for the new night club room. The walls are covered with rich black velvet, contrasting with the rich Chinese red velvet drapes at the windows. The new orchestra stand is modernistic in style. Soft shaded lights in deep red and blue are the only illumination of the stand. The wall lights are covered with painted masks, adding a bizarre and interesting touch. Al Hamilton, Memphis artist, designed these masks. The room itself was done by Jay Thorne and shows the smartness of New York Clubs. Gone are the two walls, long familiar to Nite Kap habitues, and the fireplace, adding much more dancing space to the former Italian room. Still there, however, are the floor lights.

"Of course the largest dinner party at the opening tonight will be the one for Debutante Virginia Bethell Symes of Denver, given by her grandparents, Mr. and Mrs. John Price Edrington. Then there'll be the dinner party for Therese Canale and her fiance, Warfield Rogers, given by Julia Marie Schwinn.

"Another dinner party has been planned for Mr. and Mrs. A.M. McCarthy and Mr. and Mrs. 'Buddy' Gilbert of Electric Mills, Mississippi, with Miss Mary Elizabeth Chark as hostess. In this group will be Dr. and Mrs. J.O.Gordon. Mr. and Mrs. W.C. McCormick, Dr. and Mrs. Russell Hennessey, Dr. and Mrs. Henry Hedden, Dr. W.T. Brawn, Dr. J.J. McCaughan. Miss Chark will be escorted by F. Daly Sullivan.

"Mr. and Mrs. Jay C. Bruce, recently moved here from Jackson, Tenn., and their brother, Parker Bruce, who also has come to Memphis to make his home, will be in a congenial party. Miss Peggy Hutcheson of Jackson, Tenn., will be the guest of Parker Bruce."

These constant parties and gatherings are listed to show that the Peabody was in constant use as a social center. The Samovar Room, however was soon deemed `gloomy' and was completely redone in time for the following year's Friday `Nite Cap' season. The new Cadet Room was modernistically decorated in pink and blue with blue mirrors on the supporting columns. The season was opened by George Hamilton's Music Box Orchestra.

**The Peabody at one time had its own playing cards.**

Another, more interesting observation is attributed to Clarence Selden, who remarked that during this period (1930s), "It was possible to get anything you wanted at the Peabody. You never had to leave." In fact, some people didn't leave. George Landres, a New York merchant who moved to Memphis in 1918, and opened a ladies apparel store on Main Street, lived in the original 1869

Peabody before moving to the present hotel when it opened its doors in 1925. Except for an unsuccessful four year marriage, he lived in the Peabody until it closed in 1975, a period of slightly more than half a century.

OH, You.

COMPLIMENTS OF PEABODY CAFE. MEMPHIS, TENN.

This greeting card of a little Dutch girl was from The Peabody Cafe. The caption on the back reads 'You certainly look good with sparkling eyes of blue. Could you be true? Oh no, not you. C'est me.'

The Peabody's prosperity and fame continued to grow throughout the World War II years, despite rationing and other deprivations occasioned by the war effort. Soldiers and sailors from nearby bases were permitted to spend the night at no charge in the hotel's lobby, provided they rose early, as not to interfere with the hotel's normal operation. The Peabody's financial success continued throughout the decade. In 1948 the Peabody Orchestra was formed to play for the Sunday lunch crowd at the Venetian Room. Local as well as national bands and orchestras continued to play on the hotel's top floor at the Skyway. For a time, a vocal group consisting of hotel employees daily serenaded guests and their visitors in the lobby during the late afternoon hours from the mezzanine level. After the war, and prior to the hotel's rebirth, and the prosperity of present times, the 1940s may well have been the Peabody's zenith.

The elegant and spacious ballroom is an elegant venue for large meetings, conventions, and private parties, and weddings.

# The Peabody Ducks

**The Famous Ducks always receive red carpet treatment and live in penthouse suite. They expect and deserve no less.**

Who would even think to place ducks in the fountain at one of America's most famous hotels? And why? Actually, what started as an afternoon prank has developed over time into one of the greatest marketing ideas ever created to publicize any business. This has become the stuff of legends and ranks at the top of the marketing chain, along with Chattanooga's famous 'See Rock City.' Basically, according to tradition, here's what happened. In the past, duck hunters often used live ducks as decoys. One time, for a joke, hotel manager Frank Schutt and friend Chip Barwick put some live decoys in the hotel's fountain after a hunting trip. Supposedly they'd been drinking a bit. In any event, this amusing and totally spontaneous action generated a great deal of publicity for the hotel, and it was soon decided that the ducks should remain in the fountain on a permanent basis.

What is related above is the way the origin of the ducks in the fountain is generally agreed to have occurred, and the passage of time has hardened this account into fact. Be that as it may, it would be negligent not to mention that there was a conflicting account from a source who was very credible in his own right. A December 1967 article in the former Memphis *Press Scimitar* by staff writer Robert Johnson stated in regard to the legend of the ducks:

"There are two stories about the ducks, and there has been disagreement for many years about which is true. Many years ago I wrote one story-that the late Frank Schutt, president and general manager of the Peabody for so long, and Chip Barwick, auto dealer, had been on a hunting trip, returned feeling festive, and since this was the time when live decoys were legal, they brought back a wood duck and turned him loose in the fountain, where he immediately declared himself king.

"Later, I got a letter from A.L. Parker, veteran hotel man who had been president of the old Memphis Hotel Co., first owner of the hotel, the man who dreamed its elegance and brought it about.

Mr. Parker's penmanship was difficult to decipher, but I gathered from about five closely written, passionately-worded pages that the story was false, that he had the ducks put in because ducks and this part of the country just seemed to go together."

But the idea for the ducks may have been the result of an even earlier attempt to utilize the fountain as a wildlife refuge. A 1978 article in the *Commercial Appeal's* popular '50 Years Ago,' meaning 1928, read as follows:

"PEABODY, THE BABY alligator that swims in the pool in the Peabody Hotel lobby, is alone today. His two friends, Gayoso and Chisca, will never again join him in the ornate pool that was home for the three babies for many months. Chisca and Gayoso died yesterday at the Overton Park Zoo, where they had been taken when they fell ill last week. Children will miss them. So will some of the adult guests, especially those for whom, after indulging in 'prohibited spirits,' watching alligators takes on a special hilarity. Never fear though, two more alligator babies are on the way from Florida."

In any case, the ducks became an important and permanent feature of the Peabody.

At the end of each day, the ducks walk the red carpet back to the elevator which returns them to their 'penthouse.'

**Bellman Edward Pembroke**, once a circus trainer, offered to escort the ducks to and from the fountain. He was named

'Duckmaster,' and held that distinguished title from 1940, until his retirement in 1991. And thus a tradition which was inadvertently started, almost as a joke, continues to this day. Every morning at 11:00 a.m. sharp, the ducks, a drake and four hens, are brought by elevator from their 'penthouse' on the roof, and escorted to the fountain in the center of the lobby on a red carpet. Every evening, promptly at 5:00 p.m. the ducks depart the fountain, following their red carpet to the elevator, and ride back to their rooftop lodgings. Their brief journey is ceremoniously accompanied by marching music and cheers of approval from those gathered to witness this purely Southern tradition which has, over the decades, added to the already considerable reputation of the Peabody Hotel. Due to the initially favorable public response to the ducks, other animals were tried briefly in the fountain, including turtles and even alligators, but it was the ducks which proved most popular. Today, they are famous throughout the world. In fact, the ducks traveled to New York where they were presented with the first Lifetime Achievement Special Public Relations Award from the Hospitality, Sales, and Marketing Association International.

They've also appeared on the *Tonight Show* with former longtime host Johnny Carson, and have been honored guests at the movie premier party for the George Lucas film, '*Howard the Duck*.' Despite their international celebrity and posh lifestyle, they manage to keep their fame in proper perspective, unlike some of their human counterparts, and frequently make time for charitable events in support of a number of worthy causes, including St. Jude's Children's Research Hospital, the Audubon Society, and others. Everywhere they go they bring smiles to the faces of those who see them, just as they do when home at the Peabody.

The ducks also travel extensively to other parts of America, promoting The Peabody and other Belz properties. While on the road, they enjoy a lifestyle similar to that to which they are accustomed at the Peabody. They're always escorted by an entourage in charge of their accoutrements which include a fabulous carrying cage, their traditional red carpet, and a portable fountain for their swimming comfort. Accommodations invariably include a suite in one of the finest hotels available, whether in New York, Washington, or even Las Vegas. They always travel by jet and are never left unattended in a flimsy cardboard box at the baggage or freight loading platform of some decaying bus station. They are true celebrities, and everywhere they go, their appearance creates a sensation. People are always pleasantly surprised and happier for having seen them.

At day's end, the ducks are ceremoniously escorted through the Peabody lobby, into the elevator, and to their spacious penthouse atop the Plantation Roof. The new structure was built for them at a cost of $15,000 in 1984. It is 12 feet wide, 18 feet long and 12.5 feet tall. It was designed by Memphis artist Elinor Hawkins who had worked on the hotel's lobby ceiling and murals. The Royal Duck Palace features an Arabian roof, banners, and a six foot diameter fountain, as well as murals and a covered bed chamber.

The fountain is noteworthy in that it has a centrally placed statue of a large duck with water flowing from its bill.

This model of the Plantation House in the Royal Duck Palace was located on The Peabody's celebrated Plantation Roof, and was a smaller version of the original larger structure still found there.

**The way to the roof top Duck Palace is clearly marked.**

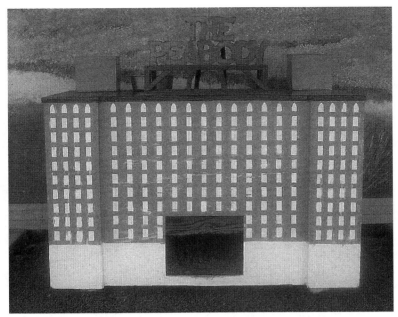

**The Ducks' 'plantation house' has been replaced by a larger model of The Peabody Hotel, as befitting their fame.**

**The Peabody Ducks** enjoy a relaxing evening dip in their private penthouse pool at the end of a hard day's work. Their earlier (1984) penthouse suite seen here has been replaced by the newer, more elegant residence.

**The Duck Palace** has been updated and is more elegant now than it has ever been, with an enclosed area which provides them four season comfort as well as stately marble surroundings.

The ducks continue to be of great significance to The Peabody, apart from their travels and daily appearances. In 1988 The Peabody Honorary Duckmaster Program was initiated. In this event someone is selected from a visiting convention or meeting, presented with the title of 'Honorary Duckmaster' given a tee-shirt and cane and allowed to lead the ducks. This activity always provides an entertaining diversion to the visiting members of any group or meeting, as well as to the hotel's guests. On occasion, a visiting celebrity may serve as guest Duckmaster. But what is truly amazing is that despite the number of times that this twice daily march of the ducks has occurred over the years, it is always a major event. Guests and visitors invariably begin gathering near the elevators and around the fountain in the morning, awaiting the arrival of the ducks. It is the same at the end of the day as preparations are made for their departure. Even the most experienced traveler is delighted by witnessing their arrival or exit.

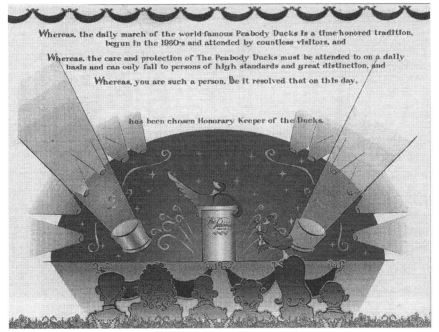

Whereas, the daily march of the world-famous Peabody Ducks is a time-honored tradition, begun in the 1930's and attended by countless visitors, and

Whereas, the care and protection of The Peabody Ducks must be attended to on a daily basis and can only fall to persons of high standards and great distinction, and

Whereas, you are such a person, Be it resolved that on this day,

has been chosen Honorary Keeper of the Ducks.

**The Duckmaster Certificate is inscribed for the honorary Duckmaster as a souvenir of the occasion.**

Former Duckmaster Kalyn Housdan prepares to return the Ducks to the Royal Duck Palace shortly before 5 PM continuing the tradition of Edward Pembroke, the first and also, the longest serving Duckmaster.

**The Peabody Duck March** is a source of joy to all who gather for both their arrival in the morning, and departure in the evening. Duckmaster Doug Weatherford is one of three duckmasters. The show must go on every day, so there is always a standby.

Duckmaster Jimmy Ogle is a successor to the original Duckmaster, Edward Pembroke, and will be found visiting with the ducks' many fans in the lobby, answering questions, and posing for pictures with hotel guests and visitors.

"It's not that we're aloof, and we're not ignoring you. In fact, we deeply and sincerely appreciate your very kind and thoughtful attention, it's just that we just have a lot of swimming to do in a rather limited amount of time. I knew you'd understand, so now it's back to work. Thanks again for stopping by. It's always nice to see you."

## ENGINEERING

Both ongoing maintenance and improvement at the hotel are constant and seemingly never ending. Beneath the surface elegance of the Peabody lobby and ballrooms there is a vast underworld of wiring, pipes, boilers, and other equipment which are vital to the operation of the hotel. Every guest expects hot water when desired, expects the phones to work, every time, and expects everything to be the best available. To ensure that this occurs, a fulltime staff of engineers and maintenance personnel are always at work. This is as true today as when the hotel was first built. A 1950 newspaper article in the Memphis *Press Scimitar* entitled `A Trip Downstairs at the Peabody' described the engineering spaces as follows:

"Underneath Hotel Peabody is a world all by itself-a world of great throbbing engines and generators, turbines, boilers, catwalks and control panels. It's something like the engine room of a battleship. Great polished wheels of the generators, eight feet tall,

119

whirl about ceaselessly pumping the thick pistons which supply power for hotel lights. A puff of white steam escapes with a hiss from one of the three high pressure boilers, great square structures that disappear 25 feet overhead in a maze of pipes, tubes, and steel walkways.

The hotel makes its own electricity, pumps its own water from two wells (450,000 gallons a day), and has its own heating and air-conditioning. In case of a city breakdown, the hotel is independent. By the same token, if the hotel equipment ever were to break down, it is hooked up with the city utilities, so the city would supply both water and current. The city is supplying part of the current now, but if the main circuit breaker is thrown, the hotel is ready to take the full load.

Charles G. Moore, 2123 Linden, assistant chief engineer, took a *Press-Scimitar* reporter on an informal tour. Mr. Moore has been working with engines almost all his life. The pipes and motors under the Peabody are clean and polished. He pointed with pride to one piece of equipment after another. One of three hot water circulating pumps, with the flywheel (at 1740 rpm) whirling around so fast it looked as if it were standing still. These keep hot water the same temperature in all parts of the hotel. Two ice water pumps, three brine pumps (for the cold storage in the kitchens). Three big ammonia compressors. Pumps for two artesian wells. Air-conditioning and vacuuming systems."

As early as 1952 the Peabody installed automatic Otis elevators as part of a $350,000. overall modernization. An automatic elevator, one where you just get on and push a button is something we all take for granted today. Prior to its advent however, an elevator attendant, usually uniformed, sat on a very small folding wood seat just inside the elevator door. He or she would manually shut the doors, then pull a floor to ceiling folding brass screen across the door opening. The elevator operator would control the ascent or descent speed with a large brass wheel affixed to the side of the elevator wall. As the elevator passed different floors you would see the closed doors of that floor through the brass grating as you passed. It was really quite an experience. Sometimes the elevator operator would overshoot the intended floor and have to backup.

The elevators jerked and lurched. It was fun. The addition of automatic passenger elevators, each with walnut paneling and indirect lighting, expedited guest movement in an atmosphere of comfort and elegance. The new passenger and freight elevators were capable of moving 400 ft. per minute on rubber rollers, had center opening doors, and a capacity of 2,500 pounds each.

**WREC Radio began broadcasting from its studio in the Peabody's basement in 1929, a relationship which endured on and off through 2008.**

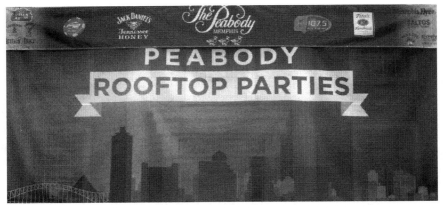

**Summer rooftop parties are a long standing and ongoing tradition at The Peabody.** The roof is one of the most enjoyable places at the hotel, and whether just walking around for a stroll or looking down at the Mississippi River, the wide open area provides a panoramic view of the city. In fact, downtown Memphis is just about the perfect size, with just the right amount of early skyscrapers, but not so many as to block the sun. And historic Beale Street is literally around the corner.

A row of new mid-1960s Buick convertibles shown parked along side The Peabody at night, no doubt provided by the local Buick dealer in support of the Bowling Association whose convention was meeting there. Note, they're all convertibles.

Why not "Hip-Hop" to the Warner often?

Buddy Fisher and The "Union"

## HOTEL PEABODY..... W·R·E·C DAILY

Memphians looked forward to the daily broadcasts which were aired live on the radio by station WREC from its studio at the Peabody. Entertainment varied as different artists were featured. The term 'Hip-Hop' as mentioned on the poster above as applied to music, is a term which existed since the beginning of the big band era, and possibly even earlier.

# Now Playing!

*"The Nation's Most Talked About Musical Personality"*

# PAUL NEIGHBORS

### AND HIS ORCHESTRA

*Featuring:*

★ CECELIA

★ THE THREE NEIGHBORS

★ RALPH ANTHONY

*The Skyway*

**HOTEL PEABODY • Memphis**

F. R. SCHUTT, President & General Manager

124

Another expensive proposition was the air conditioning of the entire hotel. This process was accomplished over a period of several years and completed in 1952, at a cost of over $250,000. The first stage was the air conditioning of all public areas, including the open lobby, mezzanine, restaurants and the Skyway. Two-250 horsepower compressors were installed in the basement to operate the system. The most difficult part of the project was the replacement of the ceilings in each of the guest rooms to accommodate the air conditioning vents. This extra expense allowed the guest rooms to be air conditioned without the necessity of having unsightly window units hanging precariously over the sidewalks below as with many older hotels.

In 1958 extensive changes in interior decor were made to some of the hotel's 625 rooms. All four of the two-story balconied suites were redecorated. A dozen corner suites and four front suites on the north side from the fifth through the eleventh floors were redone in the traditional style, but with a modern``58' touch. Another 120 rooms had the darker mahogany furniture and traditional beds, dressers, lamps, and artwork replaced with blonde contemporary furniture and modern art paintings. Even more radical styling changes were accomplished in five of the 43 salesmen's sample rooms on the third floor, where the walls were covered in plastic with designs echoed in the curtains. All furniture and lamps were replaced with ultramodern fixtures.

**This silver plated bowl was made for The Peabody by International Silver. Reed & Barton also made teapots for the hotel.**

**Reed & Barton sugar bowl**

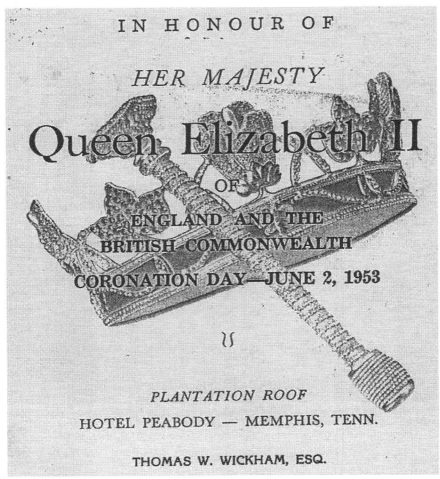

IN HONOUR OF

*HER MAJESTY*

Queen Elizabeth II

OF

ENGLAND AND THE
BRITISH COMMONWEALTH

CORONATION DAY—JUNE 2, 1953

*PLANTATION ROOF*

HOTEL PEABODY — MEMPHIS, TENN.

THOMAS W. WICKHAM, ESQ.

The coronation of Queen Elizabeth II, and a warm summer night provided as good a reason as any for an excellent dinner and celebration under the stars at the famous Plantation Roof. The

126

Menu for the royal event featured a variety of wines, SCOTCH...SCOTCH...SCOTCH and SCOTCH.' The 'Musical Interlude' included a performance of 'There'll Always Be An England As Long As Scotland's There.' Some menu items were offered in French, English and 'Southern' including Pommes au Gratin Colonial, Pois Vertes au Champignons a L'anglais, 'Limey' Beans, Rolls a la Picadilly.

**1952 Menu**

The magnificent Venetian Dining Room, located on the Mezzanine Level served lunch from Noon until 2:00 PM. There were other restaurants at the hotel as well, including the Cypress Room coffee shop, and the Colonial Room, which served breakfast and lunch daily. The Peabody Grill's Carnival Room was open 24 hours a day. Then, as now, there is something for everybody at The Peabody, from the casual to the classic.

**Another view of the elegant Venetian Dining Room.**

In addition to constant maintenance, and frequent remodeling there is the ongoing financial aspect of operating the hotel. Things took a turn for the worst in the 1950s and many grand downtown hotels suffered despite the booming postwar economy. The Peabody was no exception. In 1952 the first Holiday Inn in the world opened in Memphis on Summer Avenue. In 1953 a second Holiday Inn opened in Memphis, and tourist courts and motor lodges became the new trend nationwide. Downtown traffic and parking were no longer a problem as suburbia expanded from the strictly downtown areas and into the future. The new motels had plenty of parking right in front of patrons' rooms. There was no waiting around for valets, bellboys, or elevators. In fact, for many people, not only in Memphis, but nationwide, there was often no need to go downtown at all. By the mid-1950s a new postwar prosperity had swept the nation. Many Americans were homeowners for the first time due to the G.I. Bill. Many more Americans also had cars for the first time and moved away from cities. As they left the downtown areas for the suburbs, businesses followed. Doctors' offices, department stores, markets, theatres, all businesses which prior to World War II were almost exclusively found downtown, moved away from the cities. There were other ramifications as well. Railroads began losing passenger travel both to automobiles and airplanes. Railroad terminals had always been located in the very heart of downtown, so with the diminishing rail travel, fewer people were coming into cities, hence less business for downtown hotels. The same applied to airports. As air travel increased, hotels began springing up near airports, always located on a city's outskirts. Again, less business for downtown hotels. Soon, with revenues dropping, The Peabody was for sale.

**The new Town Park Motor Hotel**, was advertised as the Pride of Memphis, and featured 150 air-conditioned rooms, a swimming pool, and 24 hour room service, & television, in short everything of the best hotels of the era, time, without the problems of downtown traffic and the expense of parking.

PARK YOUR CAR AT—

# DeSoto Garage

60 YARDS SOUTH OF HOTEL PEABODY

Third St. at Gayoso                                    Phone 6-7364

THE SOUTH'S FINEST—LARGEST

C. B. BLACKWELL, *Manager*

While the Peabody Hotel had made arrangements for patrons and guests to park their cars, by the early 1950s many people did not feel inclined to pay for parking in addition to the cost of their hotel room and bell service. There were now other less expensive, more modern, and convenient options.

## THE ALSONETT ERA

The Peabody was subsequently bought by the Alsonett hotel chain in July, 1953 for $7,495,000. This group also owned Memphis' famous King Cotton, and more than 30 other hotel properties throughout the nation. In an effort to compete with the parking facilities of the new motels, Alsonett bought a parking garage in 1954 for $480.000. And yet the Peabody did not fare well under Alsonett's management. Again, the revenue generated by the Peabody helped support other properties to its own detriment. Personal service to customers and the former espirit d' corps which had always characterized the employees and staff diminished as well. And there were other problems too.

The Peabody had largely escaped fires, like those which destroyed the nearby Gayoso, but in 1957, the hotel's Continental Ballroom sustained in excess of $100,000 damages in a fire. Another major fire in February, 1962 began in an exhaust fan in the engine room and damaged 25 rooms to the extent that they were temporarily unusable. Other minor room fires were started by smokers, while more, small fires originated in range vents and engineering spaces. While nobody was killed or even seriously injured in any of these fires, they cast a bad light on the public's perception of the hotel's safety and security.

But an even greater injury to the hotel was about to occur. Frank Schutt, the Peabody's only manager since its 1925 reopening, retired in 1956, a further blow to the hotel. To the Peabody's friends and patrons, he and the hotel were one and the same. He had been responsible for the famous ducks in the fountain, the summer dances on the roof, the construction of the Skyway, and many other things which were so much a part of the Peabody. He was basically irreplaceable. Schutt was remembered fondly in a 'Tribute to the Hotel Peabody' during the height of his reputation as hotel manager of The Peabody:

"........Mr. Schutt has achieved a high place, and has a reputation for astuteness and keen business acumen among hotel men. This is tempered with a sweetness of character, graciousness and a sense of fairness that combine to make him beloved among his employees and a firm and true friend to his fellowmen. His friends are legion. And as he constantly adds new friends, these too remain to admire and respect for his sense of justice, fair play and ability to succeed."

Despite problems, the Peabody remained headquarters for the Cotton Carnival and other long term conventions and meetings.

"The South's Finest—One of America's Best"

# HOTEL PEABODY
(AN ALSONETT HOTEL)

## *Welcomes*

MRS. VERA BRADSHAW
of
Household Magazine

to the Opening of Cotton Carnival
May 11, 1954

★

Your Host
MEMPHIS CHAMBER OF COMMERCE

## Cocktails and Buffet Dinner

LOUIS XVI

TUESDAY, MAY 11, 1954 — 5:30 P.M.

An Alsonett era crest matchbook cover from Peabody's time under Alsonett ownership.

## An Alsonett Era Menu

So competition from other hotels, newer motels, the loss of the hotel's longtime manager, mismanagement from the hotel's new ownership, and fire, all combined to take their toll on the Peabody's fortunes during the 1950s. Other internal changes caused further loss of local patronage. The hotel management closed the basement coffee shop in 1955, a Memphis tradition, and rented the entire basement to television station WREC, for use as its television studio. The Cadet Room, the Peabody's most popular lunchroom was shut down and the space rented to the Petroleum Club. Then, in 1957, the hotel's elegant and famous dining facility, the Venetian Room was permanently closed. This Memphis landmark was famous all over the South and its closing likely angered and offended local patrons. It probably seemed to many Memphians that the hotel's management was almost trying to run people off. Other significant social changes had taken place which further diminished the Peabody's financial status. Fast food restaurants and drive-ins had become increasingly visible on the national landscape, and in Memphis too. Students from Ole Miss, Southwestern, and Memphis State, now sought social life and entertainment in places other than the Peabody. Music had also changed drastically, and Memphis, with its Sun Records, was in the forefront of the American music revolution. The orchestras and bands of the `20s, `30s, & `40s, those which had once filled the Peabody's Skyway and Plantation Roof were now obsolete, and the large formal parties, the type so frequently held at the Peabody in the past, had become much less common.

**The 1959 Les Passees `Crystal Ball' was held at the Peabody.**

The growing trend towards modernism was reflected in every aspect of American life. From fashion, to space age appliances, and furniture, to streamlined futuristic cars which resembled rockets and spaceships, everything was moving quickly away from classicism. Antique furniture, giant houses, and large hotels like the Peabody were no longer considered to be grand and elegant, but rather old and obsolete. In 1958, the Downtowner Corporation opened a modern 120 room hotel on Union, right across the street from the Peabody, providing a modern downtown hotel with free parking. Other, newer and more convenient motels soon opened in Memphis, including the Admiral Benbow on Union, a Howard Johnson's near the airport, and another Holiday Inn.

The next blow the hotel faced was integration. It opened its doors to black patrons in 1961, but the move was not without consequences. Memphis was then a highly segregated city, and socialites of the era were not prepared to accept such radical changes literally (they felt) overnight. The loss in revenue was immediate. In the 1961-1962 year the Peabody lost $245,700 in profits. The next year saw a further drop of $78,000. Basically the hotel was abandoned by the Memphis upper crust as a result of its inclusive policy toward blacks. But the hotel and the black population of Memphis had always had a close bond. Of the hotel's approximately 900 permanent employees in 1951, 650 were black and many had positions of great responsibility. While it would be incorrect to say that racial prejudice did not exist in the South, or even in the Peabody, the hotel did promote blacks. Hosea Wright the Peabody's 44 year old executive chef, spent 28 years at the hotel prior to its bankruptcy. He started as a dishwasher, then became coffee maker, short order cook, roast cook, first cook, chef's steward, and finally executive chef. In any case, the Memphis bon ton felt forced to look elsewhere for a place to hold their meetings and parties. Newer hotels and motels opened, and for a time sufficed, but none of these newer facilities possessed the grace, charm, or traditions of the Peabody. Ultimately, everybody lost.

**Beale Street's Hotel Clark** While much has been said by historians about black patrons being denied service at ʻwhite hotels,' most so-called ʻblack hotels' of the era were every bit as exclusive and discriminatory as their counterparts. ʻColored Only' restaurants and hotels were common in most major cities in the North and South in the pre-civil rights era, largely created, owned, and operated by successful black entrepreneurs.

But it wasn't just integration which brought the Peabody to its knees, it was the many changes occurring in the South. The agricultural economy had been largely replaced by a faster paced business world. Edward Pembroke, the Peabody's original Duckmaster, and superintendent of hotel services summed it up this way: "Farming's gone, the salesmen travel by plane, come in here and do a million dollar's worth of business and go back the same day. Everybody's giving free parking and this (The Peabody) is just not built for that. It's common sense."

In addition to substantial lost revenue, the hotel was faced with massive debts, including a first mortgage in excess of $2,000,000 owed to the Equitable Life Assurance Society of America, another $337,500 to the Memphis National Bank of Commerce, and $876,199 due to former stockholders as a third mortgage. Add to these figures interest debts of $175,000 and past due taxes of $95,000 and it's easy to see why The Peabody was in trouble.

By 1965 it was over for the Peabody, at least for the moment. Attempts to refinance and reorganize the hotel's debts failed and Judge Bailey Brown approved plans for a foreclosure sale. Delta Auction Company was chosen to conduct the sale and an auction date was set for Tuesday December 14, at noon at the Shelby County Courthouse. Delta at that time had offices in Ft. Worth, Houston, Dallas, Baton Rouge, and New Orleans as well as executive offices in Memphis.

**FORECLOSURE SALE**

HOTEL PEABODY

TUESDAY December 14th
12:00 NOON
SHELBY COUNTY
COURTHOUSE
Memphis, Tenn.
PRELIMINARIES 11:00 A.M.

Delta Auction Co. Inc.
Executive Offices
1254 Lamar Avenue Memphis, Tenn. 38104
Phone 274-7817
LICENSED BONDED INSURED

**The Beautiful Peabody
468,000 SQUARE FEET
OF A GREAT HOTEL**

FULL DETAILS INSIDE

**The Foreclosure Sale of the Hotel Peabody was indicative of the continuing deterioration of downtown areas nationwide due to flight to the suburbs by businesses and retail shops. This flyer announced the auction of the Memphis landmark.**

As is common in cases where an expensive and nationally known property is to be auctioned, an informative and detailed brochure was compiled about the hotel which was mailed to

139

interested parties. The auction brochure is a true collectible piece of Memphis memorabilia. It was very detailed and sought not only to present the hotel in its most favorable light, but to portray the City of Memphis as `...the second fastest-growing city in the entire South.' To that end a series of facts about both the hotel and Memphis were cited. As regards Memphis itself, the following points were made in the brochure:

* Metropolitan Memphis has a population of more than 800,000 and is just beginning to burst into full growth
* Memphis has four lifelines, river, rail, motor and air, that link it with the big and growing markets throughout the South, the Southeast, the Southwest and the Midwest.
* Memphis is in the heart of one of America's richest agricultural regions.
* Eight railroads serve 25 states from Memphis. Seven bus lines and 89 motor freight lines are established in Memphis. Seven airlines operate more than 160 in and out flights daily.
* Annual retail sales have topped the $841,000,000 mark. Memphis' trade area is composed of more than eight million people with effective buying income of more than $12 billion.
* As a major river port, Memphis is near the center of the great Inland Waterways System. More than 7,000,000 tons of river cargo are handled annually by the Port of Memphis. Four barge lines serve the city.
* The new Memphis Memorial Stadium is the largest structure of an all-new sports complex at the Fairgrounds. The 50,000 seat stadium was built at a cost of $3,650,000. The sports complex also includes a new $5,500,000 Mid-South Coliseum with a seating capacity of 12,000.
* Memphis boasts the South's largest Medical Center. Recent improvements include a new Tennessee Psychiatric Hospital and Research Institute, additions to Baptist, Methodist and St. Joseph's Hospitals, new facilities for the University of Tennessee

Medical Units, new Baptist Medical Building, J. K. Dobbs Medical Research Institute, W.F. Bowld Hospital and a new St. Jude's Hospital, spearheaded by comedian Danny Thomas. A new Veterans' Hospital is under construction.

* Downtown Memphis has taken on a new face, with the addition of new buildings. Many are finished, others are under construction. A downtown airport is in operation one minute from Main Street. Ten minutes from downtown is a $50,000,000 President's Island Harbor Project, a great, thoroughly-planned industrial park with river, rail, and motor transportation.

* A new $21,000,000 jet-age airport is in use. Traffic is now using part of a new $162,600,000 expressway system. Shopping centers, new subdivisions, and dozens of apartment buildings are going up. A major urban renewal program is under way.

* Memphis has passed all tests for plant locations. Locally organized and financed industries and national firms are prospering here, and many are expanding. There are about 800 manufacturers in Memphis, with industrial employment ranging up to 50,000.

The hotel's strong points were was described just as thoroughly as the city's:

'The Peabody is truly a tradition in hotel keeping and a great landmark in the Mid-South. One of America's well-known authors once wrote "The Delta of the Great Mississippi River starts in the Lobby of the Peabody Hotel in Memphis." The present building was constructed in 1924, by a most thorough hotel man and has one of the best hotel layouts in America. Built with no regard for expense, with architectural detail, layout and appointments far ahead of its time, the hotel for many years returned extremely satisfactory profits to its owners.'

141

This was followed by a more detailed description of the hotel in bold type:

## `A FEW FEATURES OF THE HOTEL-FAMOUS AS `THE SOUTH'S FINEST AND ONE OF AMERICA'S BEST'

* THE PEABODY is the Mid South's largest hotel and occupies a half-block in the heart of busy bustling downtown Memphis---an area that is being speedily revised. A new Civic Center is under construction and among the new buildings are a City Hall, Federal Building, State and County Office Building. Two new office buildings have been finished, one is 38 stories. A 24-story department store and apartment complex, plus many new stores and other apartments are being built. A Convention Center and Exhibit Hall are planned--- all of which add to the future importance of the Peabody Hotel.
* THE PEABODY'S thirteen story building contains 468,000 square feet of space, is AIR CONDITIONED, and equipped with television, radio and Muzak.
* THE PEABODY has 625 large, comfortably arranged guest rooms; 15 meeting and banquet rooms, 8 office spaces and the famous Petroleum Club on the mezzanine, plus 42 well-appointed rooms available for sales meetings and exhibits on third floor.
* THE PEABODY ballroom seats 750 for meals and 1,000 for meetings, when used in conjunction with the adjoining Louis XVI room.
* There are three restaurants on the ground floor. The Skyway supper club is located atop the hotel and there is an open roof for summertime dancing and dining.
* THE PEABODY has long been recognized as the CONVENTION CENTER OF THE MID-SOUTH, and is the largest convention hotel in Memphis. All of the airlines who have downtown offices are in the Peabody; limousines serving all airlines leave from the Peabody. It is a focal point of the business

and social life of the area.

A picture of the Skyway was described as follows: `The Skyway seats 580 for meals or meetings. The Skyway is probably the most romantic dining and dancing setting in the nation. Hotel Peabody music broadcasts have originated here for more than a quarter of a century.'

A photograph of the Continental Ballroom was accompanied with the caption: `Continental ballroom, seats 750 for meals. 1000 can be seated for meetings in conjunction with the Louis XVI room.'

A typical guest room was pictured in another photograph. `All 625 guest rooms have air conditioning, television, and radio. All are comfortably arranged.'

Finally, Delta Auction Co. valued the property as follows:
REAL ESTATE- 62,275 Square feet at $19.26 sq. ft.-$1,200,000
BUILDING-468,000 Sq. ft.-$4,600,000.
FURNITURE AND FIXTURES-$992,000.
EQUIPMENT AND MACHINERY-$ 712,000.
TOTAL-$7,504,000.

Additional inventory included accounts receivable, food and cigar stand inventories, televisions, chinaware, glassware, silverware, linens, blankets, fuel oil. Engine room supplies and other operating supplies consumable in use are not included in this sale.

An `ALL-STAR CAST OF PERMANENT TENANTS' was listed in the brochure announcing the auction as follows:
Memphis Chamber of Commerce
WREC Radio and TV (CBS Memphis Outlet)
American Airlines Ticket Office
Braniff Airlines Ticket Office
Delta Airlines Ticket Office
Civitan Club Headquarters

Kiwanis Club Headquarters
Rotary Club Headquarters
Associated General Contractors
Gray Line Tour Service
Cotton States Fashion Exhibits
Petroleum Club Headquarters
Drug Store
Photo Shop
Men's Shop
Fine Tailor Shop
Florist
Letter & Steno Service
Fine Jeweler
Coin Exchange
Liquor Store

A disclaimer was enclosed which stated that 'The information contained in this brochure was derived from sources believed to be correct, but it is not guaranteed. All financial data was obtained from records of Memphis Peabody Corporation and Hotel Peabody Company, or their predecessors.'

Delta Auction Company maintained an office in room 203 of the hotel until December 14, so that representatives would be on hand at all times to take prospective buyers around the hotel or to provide information to interested parties. Advertisements were placed in major newspapers throughout the nation alerting the public to the hotel's impending sale. As news of the upcoming event spread, people and organizations, including representatives from hotel chains, investment groups, and wealthy private citizens traveled to Memphis to inspect the hotel property. It was speculated among prospective buyers that an initial investment of about $5,000,000 would be required to buy the hotel, pay all of its debts, delinquent taxes, restore it to its former grandeur, and update it to modern standards as a hotel and convention center.

Despite the sad state of affairs the Peabody was in at the time, the general consensus in Memphis, was that someone would buy the hotel and that it would be open again soon under new management. There may have been some doubt that the hotel would again regain its former status, but there was little doubt that the Peabody would be open forever. It was an integral part of Memphis life.

Ultimately, the sales brochure proclaimed in bold black letters: `Someone is going to get a REAL BARGAIN on December 14th' `THE QUEEN OF THE NATION'S HOTELS, the South's finest and one of America's best, is going to be sold through foreclosure proceedings. Someone is going to get a great hotel for a fraction of its real value---and it might as well be you!

`THE PEABODY HOTEL sold in 1954 for $7,500,000 or exactly $12,000 a room. If a buyer were able to purchase this property in the $3,500,000 to $4,000,000 range----this would bring the cost per room, down to the $5,600 to $6,400 range.

`AND THE BARGAIN IS EVEN GREATER because present commercial rentals, on sound leases, currently produce over $150,000 per year. If this income were capitalized at ten times, and considered worth $1,500,000, it would reduce the cost per room by another $2,400---which makes the hotel cost, per room, particularly low.'

The public auction was held on a chilly December 14 at the courthouse steps as a crowd of more than 1,000 gathered to witness the historic event. A festive atmosphere prevailed despite the shadow cast over the proceedings by the presence of the cold, and the overcast sky.

(Photo used by permission of Anna Olswanger)

Live Dixieland jazz provided by Berl Olswanger's band entertained the crowd as members of the press, including television and newspaper reporters from across the land gathered to report the results of this highly publicized and historic sale.

Opening remarks were offered by James Pirtle of the Chamber of Commerce, and Commissioner James Moore, who addressed the waiting crowd with the words, "You're not buying a hotel today, but a glorious tradition." An opening bid of $2,000,000 was offered by Hoyt Wooten, whose WREC-TV studios were located in The Peabody. He had handed a deposit check for $300,000 to one of the auctioneers prior to the bidding. There were several qualified buyers on hand, including Holiday Inn founder Kemmons Wilson, and Otto Mueller, owner of the nearby Tennessee Hotel. Neither bid, however. After two time outs and more waiting around, the hotel finally sold for $2,300,000 to an Arkansas businessman Robert Bogardus Snowden, far less than the nearly $7,500,000 paid by Alsonett in 1954. It should be mentioned that the original Peabody had been given to Snowden's grandmother as a wedding present. Snowden also had prior experience with the Peabody, having been a part owner prior to its sale to Alsonett. Snowden immediately announced plans to restore the hotel and estimated the cost to be another $3,000,000 over and above the purchase price. He said that the restoration would also include a motel and a swimming pool and speculated that the time for completion would be between one and a half and two years.

Surprisingly, the man who bought the hotel at the December 14 auction sold it to the Sheraton Hotel Corporation within 48 hours. Actually Bob Snowden saw the sale of the Peabody as an excellent opportunity to make some pocket money. Apparently he persuaded Richard Boonisar, Sheraton's senior vice president in charge of acquisition, that purchasing the hotel would be a great bargain. Snowden made an agreement with Sheraton to buy the hotel himself and then sell it to them for a profit agreed upon in advance. Had a major company like Sheraton actually participated in the bidding, the final price would likely have been much higher. Though the purchase amount was not made public, the move was considered to have been a good one for the hotel. Everybody knew the wealth and power of Sheraton. There was no doubt now that the Peabody would be restored to its former glory. And yet there were concerns among many Memphians that the hotel might be transformed into some modern chrome and glass monstrosity, rather than simply restored. These fears were quickly put to rest by a weighty pronouncement from noted Memphis psychic who stated authoritatively, "No, they wouldn't do that."

Immediately a top management team flew to Memphis from the Sheraton company's headquarters in Boston. Architects, engineers, and decorators under the direction of Richard Boonisar set up shop in The Peabody. An interesting incident happened to Boonisar, who despite his prominence, was evicted from his room almost as soon as he arrived, in order to accommodate an Ole Miss fan who had reserved the room three weeks earlier for the Liberty Bowl game with Auburn. So The Peabody had a full house its first weekend under the new ownership of Sheraton, a circumstance considered to be a good omen.

Sheraton had previous experience with grand hotels, and already owned the St. Charles in New Orleans, and the Jefferson in St. Louis. In New Orleans, the St. Charles was revered as much as the Peabody was in Memphis. The St. Charles Hotel, located a block off Canal Street, was the third St. Charles (the first two had burned) and had roots back to the 1850s. Other than the long gone St. Louis Hotel, it was the most famous hotel New Orleans had ever known. Sheraton officials addressed and calmed any fears that the Peabody would be anything other than it had ever been. The plans undertaken by the new owners sought to restore the hotel to its 1925 appearance. The lobby, mezzanine, and ducks would remain unchanged.

A problem for Memphians, as it had been for St. Louis and New Orleans residents, was the use of 'Sheraton' in front of the hotel's actual name. Thus The Peabody was now to be called the Sheraton-Peabody, a very unpopular decision as far as locals were concerned. Sheraton reasoned that since it was footing the bill, it should receive top billing, and it did, literally. As soon as possible the massive 'Hotel Peabody' neon block lettered sign on the hotel's roof was replaced with 'Sheraton Peabody' with the Sheraton name positioned above Peabody. And despite objections, hotel operators began answering the phone, "Good morning, Sheraton-Peabody" on the morning of December 16, 1965. The fears and displeasure of Memphians were not without foundation. I saw a large banner from the Sheraton period at an antique store several months before this book was finished. It had large pictures of ducks as well as the wording 'Sheraton-Home of the Famous Ducks.' There was no reference to the Peabody name at all.

**Memphians weren't happy with `Sheraton' above the Peabody name, but in fairness to Sheraton, they restored the hotel at great expense after buying it in 1968.**

Sheraton had purchased the historic Peabody with the intention of making it a commercially successful property. Anytime any company purchases an unsuccessful business which had once dominated its market, there is always the feeling that whatever problems have come to exist in the interim can be identified and corrected, and the business can once again reign supreme in its field. If the perception existed that the Peabody could not be made profitable, Sheraton would not have purchased it at all. In the case of the Peabody, there were obvious reasons for the hotel's declining income. The physical building had been allowed to deteriorate as had the level of quality and service. There was probably mismanagement as well. The first order of business was to identify these problems, make appropriate changes, and then determine the ideal position of the Peabody in the current market atmosphere. If the hotel could be made profitable it would be more than just a moneymaker. It would be a prestigious and impressive jewel in the Sheraton crown.

Physical restoration of the entire hotel began immediately with one floor at a time closed and all rooms completely refurbished. All beds, mattresses, and furniture were replaced. The carpets were also replaced and the walls were painted in the halls on each floor. Of special interest were the hotel's two luxury suites, the French Royal Suite, and the Presidential Suite. Each of these were completely refurbished and contained a living room, bedrooms, and a dining room. The French Royal Suite was decorated with $40,000 in French antiques, making it even more luxurious. These suites, when completed, would rent for $75 per night. Four other significant, but lesser suites, known as the Romeo and Juliet Suites because of their balconies, were also redecorated.

The original terrazzo floor tiles in the main lobby were replaced with dazzling white marble and covered with elegant new rugs. The delicately carved wooden beams and scrollwork throughout the lobby and mezzanine areas were restored to their original colors. Reference to period photographs aided in the restoration not only of the lobby and mezzanine areas, but also of the meeting rooms and the original Continental Ballroom. Indeed everything was made to resemble as closely as possible the hotel's 1925 appearance. Executive offices were restored and a new Falstaff Room restaurant was added with the look and feel of an English tavern.

A hotel consulting and research firm had previously determined that the Peabody's success depended on its ability to generate constant convention business, an ability which had diminished in recent years due to lack of adequate facilities, insufficient national promotion, and restrictive liquor laws. But even the best facilities could not offset the changing social landscape and the nationwide move to the suburbs. In this sense, the problems faced by the Peabody as a downtown hotel were not dissimilar to those faced by any historic hotel in any downtown location in any major city in America. But Sheraton had a massive sales and promotional infrastructure already in place, as well as an aggressive and focused management team. By utilizing its market power, it felt that it could adequately publicize and promote the Peabody nationwide and overcome many of these problems. Additionally, Sheraton had a long standing company-wide policy of discounting room rates to military and government personnel, tour groups, corporations, students and others. These factors in conjunction with the physical restoration of the building promised a bright future.

Internally, a decision had been made to retain Martin McNeil, the hotel's manager under the Alsonett banner, as well as the rest of the hotel's current employees. In addition to the Peabody's upper management, new staff and sales members were brought in with degrees in hotel and restaurant management. Also, nearby property was purchased which allowed parking for 250 cars. Finally, after more than $2,000,000 in restoration costs, and a year and a half, The Peabody was again ready to resume its role as the pride of the Bluff City. Although the hotel had never been closed during the restoration, a grand reopening ceremony was set for March 7, 1968. Among those in attendance were the Sheraton's president, Ernest Henderson III, as well as several other of the company's top executives. Memphis mayor Henry Loeb used the Sheraton 'Golden Shears' to cut a 12 foot ribbon stretched across the Hotel's Union Avenue entrance. Members of the press and other guests were presented with parchment scrolls describing the hotel's many improvements and escorted on tours of the newly restored hotel.

The Peabody's marble fountain, is the centerpiece of the lobby, and where the ducks pass their days, much to the great delight of The Peabody's guests and visitors.

Glowing national, as well as local newspaper reports proclaimed the Peabody to be as great as it had been in its prime. The Sheraton Corporation was equally praised for having the foresight and commitment to undertake such an important and expensive project. The Peabody restoration was considered by preservationists and advocates of downtown areas to be an excellent example of how significant historical properties could remain profitable in their original usage. And yet, Sheraton had spent more than $2,000,000 at a time when motels and tourist courts were replacing downtown hotels, especially older ones. Many wondered both privately and in public, whether the hotel would be successful financially. At first it appeared that it would. Stanley Cox, Sheraton's Director of

Domestic Hotel Operations stated proudly that in January-February 1969 the Sheraton-Peabody had a 30% improvement in occupancy over January-February 1968, and 38% over the same period in 1967.

But much of what Sheraton had undertaken did not come to fruition as planned. Despite the extensive restoration of the hotel's convention and exhibition spaces, they were in no way enlarged to handle an increased capacity. Furthermore, the Skyway, which had been the entertainment showplace of Memphis during its heyday, continued losing nearly $50,000 a year, and was by 1966, open only on weekends. It would soon close for good.

Additionally, the assassination of civil rights leader Dr. Martin Luther King in spring, 1968, had cast a silent pall upon the city.

A 1971 thesis by Mary Ann Strong Connell entitled 'The Peabody Hotel' was somewhat prophetic at the time:

"With convention business increasing and profits on the rise, a new era of prosperity seems to be dawning for the Peabody. Sheraton-Peabody personnel-intelligent and efficient-are capably adjusting the hotel to rapidly changing times and directing policy toward making the Peabody a part of the new Memphis as she was of the old. With the program of 'restoration to former grandeur' complete, the Peabody will continue to serve the public pleasantly and profitably for many years--but former grandeur is an illusive term with different meanings for different generations. To the Memphians of the 'twenties and Deltans of the 'thirties, the Peabody no longer holds its special charm. The biggest and best at the right place and the right time, this hotel was a product of its environment. It thrived in an era of dollar cotton, gracious living, and social splendor: however, as times changed, so did the Peabody. Today a new generation will chart its future course, but as an institution symbolizing a former way of life, the 'South's finest and one of America's best' is now only a legend of the past."

While it was true that the era which had spawned the Peabody was gone, there was no reason to believe that the hotel could not remain successful. It had been completely restored and was now in excellent physical condition. It was understandably promoted as an elegant place, and remained the hotel of choice for those visiting downtown Memphis. It was always filled during Cotton Carnival, the week long annual festival in May. One night during May, 1973, the annual Plantation Party was hosted by the Krewe of Memphi, an old fashioned dance and show of the type held on the roof of the hotel before the Skyway was built. A new dance floor was placed on the roof's flat surface and entertainment was provided under the stars by singer Marguerite Piazza, her three daughters, and an orchestra. For a night, it seemed like old times.

Despite occasional returns to past glory, matters had not turned out well for the elegant Peabody after all, despite the large financial expenditure by Sheraton. In December, 1973, the Sheraton-Peabody closed without notice, a practice common with large companies when a decision has been reached at the executive level. Nobody in Memphis could fault Sheraton for its lack of commitment. The company had spent everything necessary to restore the hotel to its former physical condition. Its dedication had been absolute, but the decision had been made to cut its losses and move on. The inexorable march of commercial businesses and monied residents away from downtown Memphis had made the Sheraton-Peabody unsustainable financially. In short, there was little reason for any tourist or businessman to stay downtown any longer than necessary to conduct whatever business there was left to conduct. It wasn't the fault of Memphis per se, it was a reflection of the times. The rail systems which had literally connected almost every city in America with passenger trains were over by 1973. There were still active commuter lines in the northeast, but rail travel as it had existed for individual passengers was a thing of the past.

**The Governor's Suite in the mid-1970s featured a decorative style that was current at the time.**

It is a sad fact that often both companies and individuals sometimes invest large sums of money restoring a historic commercial building with the intention of making it profitable once again, either in its original purpose or in another, and still, after great time and expense, it cannot be made self-sufficient. The same often applies to persons or companies restoring antebellum or early twentieth Century mansions with the intention of repurposing them as restaurants, hotels, or bed & breakfast facilities. The cost overruns are almost always excessive, it is often difficult to find competent workers, and sometimes the original concept was insufficiently considered at the outset. The sometimes irresistible lure of owning a significant historic property often turns into a financial undertow that can drag good intentions into a sea of debt. And yet, such efforts, even when unsuccessful commercially, do preserve a historic property for another few decades, property that might not have survived otherwise.

The hotel was purchased by James Lane, an Alabama hotelier in

January, 1974, for $1,078,000, but was placed in bankruptcy on March 31, the same year, and closed at the end of the following business day, April 1. With just 53 registered guests out of a total of 617 available rooms, the hotel simply could not make ends meet. An April, 1975 article in the Memphis *Press Scimitar* lamented the hotel's sad circumstances and suggested that the city's leadership "turn its attention to keeping the Peabody open as a modern and profitable downtown enterprise."

**A section of the presidential Suite as it appeared in the mid-1970s. Note the size of the TV in the corner.**

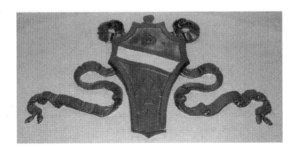

It was speculated in early 1975 that Sheraton might actually tear down the hotel altogether. Sheraton officials would not comment. What was certain was that during that very period Sheraton was dismantling the famous 804 room Sheraton-Gibson Hotel in Cincinnati. The famous St. Charles in New Orleans wasn't long for the world either. The words of a Memphis hotel and motel appraiser did not inspire confidence when he said that "...the Peabody is only worth the land it's sitting on."

Almost immediately the Memphis Chamber of Commerce, Tennessee Governor Ray Blanton, and Memphis mayor Wyeth Chandler began trying to find a way to keep the hotel open. Governor Blanton, despite his interest in saving the property, indicated that the state was not in a position financially to purchase the hotel. He suggested perhaps using some of the hotel's convention and exhibition areas for state office space, or maybe renting those and additional spaces as extra classrooms for Shelby State Community College. But members of the Chamber of Commerce felt that the hotel could not function as a landmark hotel with its banquet rooms and other areas being used in any capacity other than as part of the hotel. It seemed a no win situation and no solution was forthcoming.

ITT-Sheraton still held a $1million plus mortgage on the hotel, and sought permission to take the hotel out of bankruptcy and foreclose. This request was granted by federal bankruptcy referee William Leffler and the hotel was sold at auction on July31, 1975. It was speculated that Sheraton officials would buy the hotel, pay its debts and sell it to someone else later, but it was reported that nobody from Sheraton even attended the sale. The hotel's buyer was Ray Shainberg, acting as trustee for an undisclosed principal.. He bought the hotel for the amount of $400,000 and a few minutes later, during a competitive bidding, purchased all the hotel's furnishings for an additional $150,000.

The undisclosed principal turned out to be Belz Investment Company, Tennessee's largest real estate developer, in partnership with Edwin Hanover, Jack Belz' father in law. While Belz was prepared to offer a substantial amount of its own money, the overall project was extensive and would require more money than the hotel had ever received. Restoration costs were expected to reach nearly $12,000,000. A substantial loan or loans would be required to finance the project. There were both public and private speculation that the hotel might not be a financially viable entity no matter how much money was spent or what steps were taken. If a company with the size and market power, and financial strength of Sheraton couldn't make the hotel a financial success, what chance did anyone else have? Simply put, this perception would have to be overcome if adequate financing was to be obtained from any source.

Plans for the renovation included reducing the number of hotel rooms from 617 to 400, thus increasing room size and creating some new suites. The projected cost of $25,000 to $28,000 per room, as expensive as it was, would still be far less than the cost per room of building a new hotel from the ground up. Immediately a group of various interests spearheaded by the Belz family and Senator Jim Sasser began seeking to add The Peabody, as it was now renamed, to the National Register of Historic Places. An application was filed by Jim Williamson of Keith Kays & Associates, which had obtained similar status for other Memphis properties, notably the Orpheum Theatre and the D.T.Porter Building, the city's first tall building. In September, 1977, The Peabody was added to that long and noble list. Being on the National Register is not a guarantee that a building will not be torn down, as some people incorrectly believe. It simply means that no federal funds may be used in a building's demolition without a review at a national level. On the other hand, being on the list officially confers a certain prestige and status which, while it may have existed informally before, becomes nationally recognized upon inclusion in the list. Being added to this list also makes the honored building, in theory at least, eligible for matching funds from the National Park Service, and offers certain tax advantages. It also, in theory, makes a property's restoration more appealing to a bank or other lending institution.

As far as funding for the Peabody project, the Belz family had been waiting for two years at the time The Peabody made the National Register. They had already invested nearly a million dollars in the project including the purchase of the hotel and a parking facility. Expenses of insurance, security, taxes, and utilities were running in excess of $20,000 per month. Something needed to happen soon if the hotel was to be saved at all.

A campaign of public awareness had been launched as soon as the hotel had been purchased. The more people who wanted the hotel saved, the better. The press were very supportive as well, with nearly weekly articles from the *Press Scimitar* and the *Commercial Appeal* keeping the Memphis landmark constantly in the public eye. The hotel hosted a $10 a person 'Return to the Peabody-a Memphis Memory' in October, 1977, an event sponsored by the Memphis Heritage Association and Ballet South. More than 700 people attended the successful benefit for Ballet South, and for an evening it was like old times at the hotel lobby.

Even ducks had been specially trained by the original Duckmaster, Edward Pembroke, and returned to the fountain for the evening. By the end of July, 1978, however, nearly three years after the hotel had been purchased by the Belz family, the necessary financing had still not been approved. A controlled sale with an admission price of $2 was announced offering much of the hotel's interior furnishings for sale to the public. The sale, handled by ABC Liquidators was set to start on July, 26, 1978. It would last two months and hopefully raise $300,000. Items for sale included 400 televisions, hotel china and crystal, beds, rollaway beds, chairs, sofas, restaurant tables, coffee tables, desks, end chairs, and assorted linens, including monogrammed blankets, new and used sheets, towels, and bedspreads. A crowd of approximately 1,800 arrived on opening day, including a large number of curiosity seekers. By the end of August, most of what merchandise still remained had been moved to the lobby. The sale ran daily, including weekends. A second sale was conducted a month later, disposing of everything that remained from the Sheraton-Peabody years.

Finally, in November, 1978, after nearly three and a half years of constant effort by the Belz Investment Company, there was a light at the end of the tunnel, and it wasn't a train. A loan commitment was signed between Belz and two Memphis banks, for $7,500,000 of the $10,000,000 needed to completely redo the hotel's interior. The deal was with First Tennessee Bank and the National Bank of Commerce, which agreed to loan the money at 8.9% for 22 years, providing certain other conditions were met. Two of these conditions were that the Federal Economic Development Agency would have to guarantee 90% of the loan, and that a third bank, lending institution, or other source, would have to supply the other $2,500,000 needed to complete the project. There were still other hoops to jump through before construction could actually start: approval of a tax reduction, approval by the city building and fire inspectors, approval of the state's historical register board, and bids from contractors capable of performing the work. This was in addition to the nearly $3,000,000 of Belz's own money already committed to the project.

So far, Belz Investment Company had absorbed all of the risks involved with the undertaking of the very difficult Peabody project. Now the company needed the help of the city to bring the restoration to completion. Belz asked that Memphis close a section of Gayoso Avenue and donate it to the hotel for parking space. This was for Belz, the deal breaker. The hotel could not operate as a modern facility without adequate on site parking. The Center City Commission, the Land Use Control Board, and the city's administration all agreed, and the Memphis City Council voted to cede the land to the hotel. But even this was not without problems for the Belz Company. If substantial renovation work was not started by October, 1979, or if the hotel ceased operation for 120 consecutive days, the land would revert to the city. Additionally, there was substantial opposition from nearby businesses who complained that closing the street would create great inconveniences. Last but not least, certain individuals and groups felt that giving public land to a private business was unfair to other individuals and businesses.

But it was not over yet. A Memphis *Press Scimitar* editorial from April, 1979, stated the following:

"So the Peabody owners have had extraordinary cooperation at every step of the way. In turn, Memphis has every right to expect prompt action by the Belz family in taking care of its end of the deal by restoring the property to its former prestige as a Mid-South gathering Place."

The cavalier attitude expressed in this ill-conceived editorial was too much. This newspaper editorial almost implied that the hotel would already be restored if only the Belz Company would just get busy and quit messing around. The fact of the matter is that the

Peabody project had required thousands of man hours, hundreds of thousands of dollars, and had been a daily problem throughout the entire period. The Belzes at this point probably wished they'd never heard of The Peabody. That the city council had agreed to close a short section of one street was nothing compared to the constant and almost insurmountable obstacles which the Belzes had faced and overcome on an almost daily basis for literally years. It wasn't costing any city council member anything personally to cede some property to The Peabody project. There was no personal financial risk to any individual council member. The whole thing had put all of the Belzes through the ringer for more than 3 1/2 years. Jack Belz took specific exception to the wording of the editorial 'It's Up to the Belzes.' He clarified his position in a graceful but forceful editorial response, indicating clearly that the Belzes had never guaranteed anybody that The Peabody project would ever be realized. He further stated:

"We are hopeful that this project will come to fruition. If however, it does not, we surely will have no apologies to make to anyone because our organization will be a tremendous loser, having devoted years of our efforts and many hundreds of thousands of dollars toward a project in which we and the community have a great interest."

Belz's response was certainly justified. He and his company had gone way above and beyond the call of duty. He understandably seemed to be saying 'Back off!'

However, there were still more hoops to be jumped through. Ultimately a complicated financing plan which in retrospect can only be described as brilliant, and unique to Memphis, was put together involving multiple entities. Ultimately $13,500,000 came from various banks, with an additional $7,800,000 from the Belz family itself. The city closed a portion of Gayoso Street and ceded

162

it to The Peabody, giving the hotel a square block, which would provide adequate parking. An additional $800,000 in improvements to the sidewalks and street lamps was provided by the city, as well as tax incentives.

With financing finally secured the restoration so long hoped for by the Belz family and dreamed of by the people of Memphis, was at last undertaken. No expense was spared. The plan to reduce the number and enlarge the size of rooms was instituted, bringing the number to a total of 468. The four famous Romeo and Juliet Suites were returned to their original grandeur with spiral staircases, fireplaces and balconies all restored. The magnificently elegant Presidential Suite was also completely refurbished. The newly enlarged standard rooms were redecorated and equipped with updated, state of the art business and telecommunications ports and outlets. The famed Plantation Roof, the Skyway, the Venetian Room, the meeting rooms, and the magnificent Mezzanine and elegant lobby were all restored with painstaking attention to detail. A new full service bar was placed at one end of the lobby, in sight of the famous marble fountain, and provides an excellent place for guests and locals to socialize. A gourmet restaurant, Chez Philippe, and others were added, as well as a sports bar and a New York style deli. A complete fitness club was created and is overseen by a fulltime athletic director. There is also an indoor swimming pool. free weights, Nautilus equipment, and daily exercise classes are offered as well as steam, sauna, massages, and tanning.

By the time it was over, and the hotel was completed, its expenses were more than twice the original estimate, and four times what the hotel had originally cost in 1925.

**This commemorative coin was minted in celebration of The Peabody's restoration and reopening. By now, the hotel's original motto, `The South's Finest, One of America's Best' had been replaced by `The South's Grand Hotel.' While both are appropriate, the latter has a better ring to it, and is certainly true enough.**

When The Peabody reopened in 1981, the public was introduced to the completed project, unaware for the most part of the detailed planning and extensive work which had taken place behind the scenes. The restoration of the hotel was, however, a massive undertaking which involved significant structural and design changes as well as input from a very large group of experts in a variety of fields, including architects, electricians, plumbers, engineers, interior decorators and designers, historians, researchers, and restaurant consultants, among others. All in all, there were a total of twenty-one consultants.

Keeping all of their efforts coordinated and focused, was a major task in itself. Before any of the restoration could begin however, the architectural plans had to be formulated. Jack Belz met with Memphis architect Jack McFarland, who had worked with the Belzes on other projects, and after an interview, selected him to oversee the restoration of the hotel. Jack McFarland was probably the most qualified architect in the South for this project, mainly because of his prior experience with hotel restoration and reconfiguration. More significantly for The Peabody project in particular, was his experience with other Memphis hotels from the same period. Specifically, he'd worked on the project which had taken the former Claridge Hotel, basically gutted it, and completely reconfigured it as an apartment building. The hotel Chisca, another large downtown Memphis hotel had also been modernized as an earlier project he'd been involved with.

For the duration of The Peabody's restoration, the project was a work in progress, not just in the sense that progress was being made, but in that plans changed frequently in many cases as the overall project advanced. As an example, Architect Jack McFarland recalls that the small but elegant Board Room for the hotel's board of directors, which is located on the Mezzanine level, was reworked on three separate occasions before it was completed. And then there were the guest rooms. The plan was to reduce the original number of rooms from more than 600 to more than four hundred, basically a reduction of almost one third, a significant number by any standard. The reason for the reduction in number was to increase the size of individual rooms. During the fifty years since the 1925 Peabody had opened, the public had grown to expect larger, more comfortable rooms. Reworking the number and size of the rooms within the finite space of the hotel presented some interesting architectural and engineering problems.

The Peabody had been constructed, as was the custom in the 1920s, of large steel beams with structural clay tile vertical walls.

The clay tile walls separating guest rooms, as a rule, were three inches thick. Then, an inch of plaster was applied on each side of the tile, producing a standard five inch thick vertical wall. Additionally, the steel beams, both vertical and horizontal were encased in structural clay tile. To complicate matters, the room arrangement was not always consistent from floor to floor. Essentially, walls were removed and smaller rooms were combined, creating a single, larger room, without altering the steel framework. This process produced its own set of problems, especially where the elaborate plaster cornices were involved. In the restoration or modernization of many older commercial buildings, existing ceiling height is often lowered by suspending a different type of ceiling from the original. In the case of The Peabody, the original ceiling height was maintained, and the original ceilings were all either repaired or replaced. But again, the plaster work was more elaborate and extensive in some rooms than in others, and some had been damaged by water over the years.

It should be mentioned at this point, that there are often conflicting numbers of rooms listed in regard to The Peabody. This is true of any historic hotel, as guest rooms are often reconfigured for other purposes, with two separate rooms, for example, joined by a new door and reconfigured as a suite. The older the hotel, the more likely one will find varying numbers of rooms listed.

The grand lobby's magnificent stained glass skylights which had been covered by one of the previous hotel's owners were uncovered, restored, and backlit, all part of the extensive work involved in restoring the public spaces to their original grandeur.

**Memphis Architect Jack McFarland** (right) was the lead architect in the restoration of The Peabody. He is seen here as President of the Tennessee Society of Architects at a meeting in Nashville in 1971.

The location of the elevators in the lobby remained the same, but all of the operating machinery had to be replaced.

**The now famous Lobby Bar.** This is one of the few times you'll see it empty. A design consultant from New York, Ellen McClusky, was hired to design the restaurant, site of the former Venetian Dining Room, as well as the lobby bar. She was certainly well qualified for the job, having done interior decorating work for many world famous hotels including the Waldorf, and the Plaza in New York, among others, and major hotels in Monte Carlo, Germany, and elsewhere.

The exterior of the massive structure was also thoroughly cleaned, removing more than fifty years of accumulated grime.

Few people realize or even considered that The Peabody originally used its own in house generators to produce the electricity it used, and only used city electricity in emergencies. By the time The Peabody was restored this time, the hotel's generators had been converted to back up use only.

**The Skyway** has been completely restored to its original grandeur and is still one of the South's preferred venues for entertainment, a private party, wedding, or celebration of any kind.

The Skyway, and the Plantation Roof were the last parts of the renovation to be completed. The configuration of the Skyway remained the same as it had been since it first opened, but there was a great deal of work done on the hotel's Plantation Roof. The original roof was of the tar and gravel type, and had over the years allowed a substantial amount of damage from water leakage. A waterproof 'super membrane' was installed which alleviated many of the problems typically associated with a flat roof.

An additional problem for the hotel in the modern era was its lack of space for conventions and meetings. Much had changed in requirements for such spaces in a fifty year period. Often convention destination choices are based upon the amount of available space a hotel can offer. In this case, The Peabody purchased the former Hull-Dobbs building at the South end of the hotel and created the Tennessee Hall, and added a second story for the Memphis Ballroom at the Mezzanine level, creating additional convention and meeting spaces. The addition in square footage for convention and meeting spaces exceeded 22,400 sq. ft.

Once again, just as in the past, many nationally famous organizations select The Peabody for conventions and meetings. Its luxurious and comfortable meeting rooms and excellent service provide the perfect location for events and gatherings. Such has always been the case. For more than forty years, until its closing in 1975, the Rotary Club held meetings there, as did the Civitans and Kiwanis Clubs. Even after the hotel had closed there were weekly requests to the Belz family to use The Peabody for organizational meetings and banquets. Permission for one such organization, the City Beautiful Commission, was granted for a 1978 luncheon inasmuch as the featured guest speaker was former First Lady, Mrs. Lady Bird Johnson a nationally recognized advocate of downtown beautification.

Interestingly enough, and despite all of the renovation and reconfiguration involved in the restoration of The Peabody, architect Jack McFarland reflects that one of the most significant practical changes in the hotel was the addition of an entrance through the back door's new parking lot. Prior to this, most guests were deposited at the Union Avenue entrance by taxi where baggage was taken by a bellhop to the front desk.

The detailed wood and plaster work of the lobby and mezzanine were returned to their original condition.

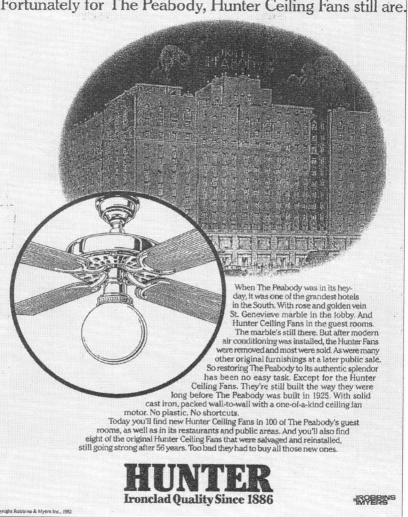

Memphis is also home to Hunter Fans, which are in their own way as much a tradition in the South as The Peabody.

**The restored lobby**

From any standpoint, the completed project was far more extensive than originally intended, but the newly restored Peabody was now far better than it had ever been in every respect, even when it was first built in 1925.

**The lobby as seen today.**

**The marble shoeshine stand**, original to the 1925 hotel, is in the basement and still open for business.

**A Free shoeshine token.**

With restoration nearing completion, a new staff was hired and trained to provide the level of personal service which The Peabody had been noted for. In July, 1981, 150 of the hotel's restored rooms were opened to the public, with the remaining 392 open to the public in August, just before the official grand reopening. With everything in place, the famous Peabody Ducks were returned to the fountain under the watchful care of Edward Pembroke, who had been responsible for them since 1940.

At last, after six years, and with the restoration now complete, The Peabody was again ready for business. There were two separate celebrations planned in honor of the completed project. The first was for 250 business, civic leaders, and friends. Each were sent invitations, the first two hundred of which were signed, numbered invitations designed by Memphis artist Dolph Smith, and printed on paper made from original Peabody linen napkins.

The second gala, the Grand Opening, was open to the public and took place on September 1, 1981. The reopening was fifty-six years to the day after the 1925 building had opened at the same Union and Third location. As might be imagined, over these two days, Peabody-style celebrations began in the morning with the arrival of Senator Jim Sasser, and Mayors Wyeth Chandler and Bill Morris in horse drawn carriages accompanied by a marching band. There were speeches from local dignitaries, members of the Belz family and others, followed by an invitation only luncheon for 300 persons at the Continental Ballroom.

The festivities continued throughout the day with a midnight champagne buffet for 450, and a grand opening dinner dance from 8-12 at the Skyway.

Trumpeter Clyde McCoy, who'd played dances at the Skyway in the 1930s again performed to the delight of both old and new patrons.

A month of celebrations including performances at the Continental Ballroom, the Plantation Roof, the Skyway, and the Venetian Ballroom featured a wide variety of legendary artists including, Burt Bacharach, Carol Bayer Sager, the Duke Ellington Orchestra, the Tommy Dorsey Orchestra, Clyde McCoy, Memphis Slim, and a host of others. There was even a musical composition to mark the event created by Dr. James Wrichens, Assistant Director of the Memphis Symphony, entitled 'The Hotel Peabody Suite.'

**The full service lobby bar.**

The full service bar offers mixed drinks and cocktails as well as a variety of bottled beers, and complimentary snack nuts and crackers. Its location at the far end of the hotel lobby makes it the perfect place for gathering with old friends or meeting new ones. In fact, the entire lobby has comfortable chairs for lounging, reading, or relaxing as well as tables with chairs and full bar service. It is the perfect choice for visitors and locals alike.

But nothing about The Peabody project had been easy. The obstacles which the Belz family had encountered from the very beginning, were way beyond anything they could have imagined even given their expertise and extensive experience in the field of commercial development. And yet their commitment met and exceeded every challenge. Only in looking back over the frequent local newspaper articles written between 1975 and 1981 can one fully appreciate the extent of their tenacity and determination. Many, lesser, and in some cases more experienced and even better financed organizations, had thrown in the towel with much less provocation. Since the original redevelopment and reconstruction of The Peabody, the Belz organization has twice additionally expanded, and added to the hotel's initial renovation. Recent major reconstruction included the expansion of the Memphis Ballroom, doubling its dinnertime seating capacity to 1,500, and extensive redevelopment of the Tennessee Exhibition Hall. Additionally, another major improvement consists of the new 'porte cochere' which can accommodate 75 cars all under cover, and a new 600 car multi-level garage which is connected by a vehicular bridge over Third Street, and an air conditioned pedestrian passage between the new garage and hotel.

Today, almost half a century after the Belz family took on the restoration of The Peabody, the hotel is everything that anybody could have hoped for, or even imagined. And indeed, it has benefited the city and served as the cornerstone and as an example for the redevelopment which has occurred in nearby areas of

Memphis. Beale Street, the Gayoso Apartments, the new baseball stadium, Peabody Place, the Gibson Guitar plant, and the upscale residential developments on the bluff overlooking the Mississippi River, all, in some measure, owe their very existence to the restoration of The Peabody. It is safe to say that Memphis would not be Memphis without The Peabody.

**Elegant marble stairways connect the basement, with the lobby and mezzanine areas and are readily accessible.**

## ALWAYS A DESTINATION OF THE RICH AND FAMOUS

Since 1869, The Peabody Hotel has always been the place to stay in Memphis. This is as true today as it was in the late 1800s, despite the presence of newer ultramodern chrome and glass hotel towers in the Bluff City. Among the important political figures who have visited or stayed at the Peabody are Presidents Andrew Johnson, William McKinley, Harry Truman, Jimmy Carter, Ronald Reagan, George W. Bush, British Prime Minister Margaret Thatcher; First Ladies Lady Byrd Johnson, and Eleanor Roosevelt, among others. Confederate generals Robert E. Lee, and Nathan Bedford Forrest. Entertainers, explorers, writers, singers, performers of all types called the Peabody home when in Memphis. Perry Como and the Ted Weems Orchestra, Jerry Seinfeld, William Faulkner, Meg Ryan, Kevin Bacon, Mike Tyson, Little Richard, Vaughn Monroe, Janet Jackson, Burt Bacharach, Susan Hayward, George Hamilton, Ann Margaret, Cary Grant, B.B.King, Jerry lee Lewis, Lou Rawls, Victor Borge, Sir Edmund Hillary, Colin Powell, Michael Jordan, Charles Lindberg, Nicholas Cage, Prince, Julio Iglesias, Mick Jagger, Yul Brynner, Queen Noor of Jordan, Dan Aykroyd, Joe DiMaggio, Johnny Cash, Carl Perkins, Joan Crawford, Dixie Carter, Dennis Quaid, Tom Cruise, Gene Hackman, Sam Phillips, Lennox Lewis, Oprah Winfrey, Lisa Marie Presley, and many, many others come to mind. Today, most famous entertainers playing larger Memphis venues like the Mid-South Coliseum, The Orpheum, the Fedex Forum, Mud Island Amphitheatre, the Pyramid, the Memphis Arena, or the main showrooms of the new casinos a few miles South, in Tunica, Mississippi, choose to stay at The Peabody. Consequently, you never know who you might see in the lobby or at one of the hotel's famous restaurants.

**A typical corner room from the 1980s.** Hotel rooms at large hotels in the 1920s were generally smaller than modern luxury hotel guests expect today. The important decision to reduce the number of rooms from 625 to 400 at the time of The Peabody's complete restoration resulted in more spacious accommodations as seen here from the mid-1980s.

**A current Executive King Room**

**Current Deluxe Double Room**

## The Restaurants of The Peabody

The Peabody Hotel has always been famous for its restaurants and unique dining facilities. During the course of the hotel's long history many changes have been made in keeping with the changing tastes of modern diners. The Peabody now features four excellent restaurants serving an extensive variety of delicious foods ranging from casual to elegant. The preparation of the hotel's legendary food takes place under the watchful eyes of two full time chefs, a pastry chef, and a dedicated staff. It is not by chance that more than half of the restaurants' patrons are Memphis locals. In a city long famous for food, this is indeed a high recommendation. The Peabody's reputation for culinary excellence is a long standing one. Frequent newspaper articles and reviews throughout the hotel's long history have praised The Peabody's fare. A 1935 Memphis *Press Scimitar* article told of a detailed model of the hotel made entirely of sugar by the pastry chef of 20 years, H. Toscano who placed the model on display in the lobby in celebration of the new Peabody's tenth anniversary in 1935.

Food preparation and presentation are an art form at The Peabody.

**The Corner Bar, upper tier.** The Corner Bar is a perfect place for a small group of friends to meet and greet in a pleasant, intimate, and unique environment with both upper and lower level seating. There is nightly live piano bar entertainment, a seemingly infinite variety of mixed drinks, as well as wine, champagne, and a nice selection of both local draft and domestic, and imported bottled and draft beers. It is the perfect location for a before, or after dinner drink, or perhaps an afternoon pick me up. In addition to the same snacks available at the Lobby Bar, the Corner Bar offers several light menu items exclusive to this venue, including chicken fingers, tenders, and wings. Should you desire something more substantial, the full menu from the nearby Capriccio Grill is always available, except on Sundays, since the Corner Bar offers its own excellent Sunday Brunch from 11:00 am to 2:00 pm. Open daily: Monday-Thursday: 4:00 pm-11:00 pm.

Friday: 4:00 pm-Midnight

Saturday: 11:00 am-Midnight

Sunday: 11:00 am-11:00 pm. **(Brunch: 11:00 am-2:00 pm)**

**Peabody Deli & Desserts** If you have a sweet tooth, there is no better place in Memphis to satisfy your craving. You may choose from a seemingly infinite selection of pies, muffins, pastries cheesecakes, rolls breads. Whatever suits your fancy is perfectly enhanced with a choice of coffees, a selection of teas, as well as bottled waters and juices, from domestic favorites to international selections. And on a hot summer day, it's hard to find anything more refreshing and satisfying than your favorite ice cream.

Hours: Monday-Thursday: 6:00 am-5:30 pm.
Friday & Saturday: 6:00 am-9:00 pm.

**Chez Philippe**, The Peabody's premier restaurant opened in 1982.

**Afternoon Tea, at Chez Philippe**

Afternoon tea at Chez Philippe is a wonderful treat and the perfect setting for an afternoon break or small celebration. Actually, afternoon tea at the hotel is a revival of an earlier tradition, but now even more elegant given the surroundings.

Chez Philippe is not only one of the highest rated restaurants in the South, but also one of the most elegant. The multi-tiered restaurant opened in 1981, and is named for Philip Belz, the patriarch of the Belz family and founder of Belz Enterprises. It lives up to its well-deserved reputation, having been honored with numerous accolades including the prestigious AAA's Four Diamond Award. It is also the only *Forbes* Four-Star Restaurant in the Mid-South, as well as one of `*Food & Wine*' magazine's Top 50 Hotel Restaurants. `*Open Table*' lists it as one of the 100 Most Romantic Restaurants in America. It's easy to understand why.

Now to the food. Chez Philippe, like many famous restaurants is offers a fixed price fare for your choice of either a four or seven full course meal. In the case of the four course meal, the diner selects one of several available choices in each of the four categories, specifically one item from Garden, Ocean, Land, and Confection (dessert). The seven course meal included a specially selected Chef's Tasting. Additional menu selections are also available such as assorted cheeses, a Caesar Salad prepared tableside, and the classic Bananas Foster, also prepared tableside. Come prepared to spend some time and enjoy the subtle and delicious flavors of a truly exceptional meal. Two things are certain: It will be one of the most memorable dining experiences of your life, and you will definitely not leave hungry. As with most exclusive restaurants, menu items sometimes change. The current menu selections are always available online, and prices for both four course and seven course meals are prominently posted at peabodymemphis.com.

Attire: Casual elegant, with jacket optional.
Hours: Wednesday-Saturday 5:00 pm-10:00 pm.
Afternoon Tea: Wed.-Sat. 1:00 pm-3:00 pm.
Reservations: 901-529-4188 or online

**The Capriccio Grill**, located just off the lobby offers a full range of menu options beginning with breakfast, including pancakes and Belgian waffles, each cooked to order, with available batter ingredients including chocolate chips, blueberries, pecans, sprinkles, and almonds, as well as extra toppings like sliced strawberries, shredded coconut, sliced bananas, whipped cream, and pretty much anything else you might want. In fact, under the 'Sweet Creations' section of the breakfast menu, the patron is addressed as follows, 'Craving something not listed? Please ask if we have it and we will gladly serve it.'

There are also any number of available individual items you can imagine including fresh fruit salad, bacon and Canadian bacon, sausage or turkey sausage, biscuits with sawmill gravy, white cheddar grits, fruit yogurts, country style potatoes, toast (white, wheat, or rye), gluten free toast, eggs any style, bagels, muffins, Danish, Croissants, and assorted cereals, and granola.

In addition to a breakfast buffet, which includes most of the above listed items, there are House Favorites like The Peabody's signature Challa French Toast, Poached Eggs on Cornbread, and their Country Burrito. There is even traditional smoked salmon on a toasted bagel with cream cheese, shaved onions, hardboiled egg, and capers. Healthy choice items are marked, and if you happen to have any food allergies, there is no need to worry. The restaurant staff is happy to modify and accommodate any dietary restrictions of food allergies.

Beverage selections include a variety of fresh juices (orange, grapefruit, apple, cranberry, and tomato), milk (whole, skim, almond, soy, or chocolate), a full range of popular soft drinks, hot tea, Cappuccino, lattes, espresso (single or double shot), spring and mineral water, and French Press Coffee. The Peabody proudly serves 100% organic and free trade certified Mayan Roast Coffee.

**SUNDAY BRUNCH** at The Peabody is served in the Capriccio Grill and is one of the most elaborate in the South, with more than 50 different sumptuous items available. The performance of live music during this time, is a tradition which began when Sunday Brunch was implemented, shortly after the reopening of the hotel in 1981.

## ACCOMMODATIONS
A variety of room selections and rates are available. Call for reservations or book online. 901-529-4000, peabodymemphis.com

## SUITES
The Peabody offers a number of magnificent suites, among which are The Abe Plough, Danny Thomas, W.C. Handy, Romeo & Juliet, and Presidential Suite. Call the main number for details or visit **peabodymemphis.com**

**Knabe Square Grand Piano.** If you're strolling the mezzanine you can't miss this magnificent square grand from the mid-1800s. It is not only massively beautiful, and exquisitely carved, but of great historic significance as well, having been made specifically for Francis Scott Key, the composer of our national anthem, `The Star Spangled Banner.' This piano is interesting for more than just its provenance. The Wm. Knabe & Co. was established in Baltimore in 1839. William Knabe was born in Kreutzberg, Germany in 1803 and moved to Baltimore in 1833, with the intention of becoming a piano manufacturer. Though he was anxious to start, he became an apprentice of inventor Henry Hartje and learned his trade while mastering the English language and accessing the business environment in America. He partnered with German piano maker Henry Gaehle producing instruments under the name of Knabe & Gaehle, an association which continued until Gaehle withdrew 1n 1854. By 1860 Knabe controlled most of the piano market in the Southern states, and this is why so many of the remaining antebellum houses still have Knabe pianos. But his company suffered from the Civil War and Knabe died in 1864. His company was taken over by his sons William and Ernest, who built it into the very successful company which it ultimately became.

**The world famous lobby is the heart of The Peabody**

The marble fountain as seen from the Mezzanine level. It is the perfect place to view the procession of The Peabody's famous twice daily duck march.

Alonsett Era Breakfast Snack Menu

**The Forest Room** is a perfect location for a wedding reception.

## MEETING, WEDDING, AND CONVENTION SPACES

If you desire to conduct a wedding reception, a trade show, board meeting, convention, class reunion, exhibition, or any other type of gathering, there is literally no better place anywhere than The Peabody. Its prestige, location, and on site amenities will transform your event from the mundane to the truly memorable. With a wide variety of meeting spaces from small capacity, intimate, and uniquely designed rooms, like the Ben Hollander Room, to the massive 16,000 sq. ft. Grand Ballroom, there is something perfect for any size or occasion. The Peabody's specialized in house staff are uniquely experienced and expertly qualified to provide a complete and full range of services including everything you could possibly want from, full audio visual, stage and acoustic setup to full catering and banquet services. And best of all...it's The Peabody. A call to the office, or an online tour of available services at **peabodymemphis.com** is the first step in creating a truly exceptional event.

191

**The GRAND BALLROOM** The Grand Ballroom's 16,000 plus square feet of open meeting space is perfect for large meetings and can accommodate a reception of 3,000 guests and or 1,250 for a banquet. It can be configured as desired into six separate sections and includes a 38' x 40' stage and 30' x 42' dance floor.

**Grand Ballroom Foyer**

**The Skyway** was restored to its original appearance by Belz Enterprises before the reopening of The Peabody, but has recently been updated acoustically and technologically while retaining its original appearance. As with the first Skyway, the dancefloor is still a significant consideration.

The 1925 Continental Ballroom's impressive marble twin stairway has long been a desirable foreground for wedding pictures. The large and elegant room also has a dancefloor and stage.

Continental Ballroom 1925 era **Continental Ballroom** The Continental Ballroom is original to the 1925 Peabody and is as elegantly detailed as it was originally. It is the perfect setting for a 700 person reception or a banquet for 350.

**Delicate wrought iron Center section of twin stairway in Continental Ballroom.**

The elegantly beautiful **Louis XVI Room** is one of The Peabody's many choices available for a private tea or luncheon.

**The Venetian Ballroom** is an elegant homage to the original Venetian Dining Room.

The **TENNESSEE EXHIBIT HALL** is the perfect location for large trade shows and conventions. With more than 11,000 sq. ft. of floor area it can accommodate 46 10' x 10' exhibit booths, and may be configured for theatre seating for 450 or classroom seating for 230 persons.

**THE PEABODY EXECUTIVE CONFERENCE CENTER** is the perfect location for a company board of directors meeting and offers a variety of spaces which may be configured as desired, from 300 to 1,100 sq. ft.

**Ben Hollander Room.** One of the favorite meeting rooms at The Peabody is the Ben Hollander Room, named for a famous bartender at the 1869 Peabody Hotel. Its dark oak paneling and leaded glass windows immediately call to mind the interior of an English great house. As you stroll the mezzanine level you will notice names on meeting room doors like Alonzo Locke, Edward Pembroke, and Frank Schutt, and others. These names are not arbitrary but exist to honor the contributions of these men to both the current 1925, Peabody and also the original 1869 Peabody.

**Third & Madison looking South, The Peabody in the distance.**

The Peabody's richly paneled Memorabilia Room, with its slightly coffered ceiling, is on the Mezzanine level, and is a relaxing place to view some of the many artifacts from The Peabody's fabled history.

The **SKYWAY & ROOFTOP**-are the perfect setting for a reception for 700 or banquet for 400.

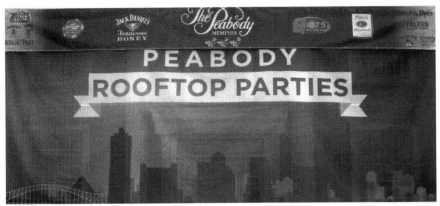

**The Rooftop Tradition continues.** On Thursday nights from Spring until early Fall, there is a very popular event on the famed hotel rooftop called 'Sunset Serenade,' in which large numbers of young people meet and socialize in a unique environment, overlooking the sparkling lights of Memphis at night.

## GUEST SERVICES

The Peabody now, as in the past, has everything you need in house, including *Feathers*, a European style spa, and *The Peabody Athletic Club.*

## *FEATHERS*

Feathers offers a full range of **massage services** for both singles and couples including express, one hour, and one and a half hour massages, including deep tissue, hot stone, relaxation, chair, prenatal, sports, ashiatsu, and Zents four handed. Available **facial services** are available for both men and women and include basically anything you could imagine from deep cleanse, cryo-collagen destressing, and more. Makeup, Hair, wax treatments, and nail services are available as well.

## THE PEABODY ATHLETIC CLUB

The Peabody Athletic Club has a variety of equipment available for strength and cardiovascular training, or just relaxing. There are an indoor swimming pool, whirlpool, Stairmaster, treadmill, free weights, Cybex equipment, elliptical crosstrainers and rowing machines. Personal training is also available as are yearly memberships for locals.

Hours: Monday-Friday
        5:30 am-10:00 pm
        Saturday-Sunday
        7:00 am-9:00 pm

## BELZ ENTERPRISES

Belz Enterprises began in the 1940s when company founder Philip Belz developed six acres in north Memphis into a warehouse complex. From these humble beginnings more than half a century ago, Belz Enterprises has developed into one of the largest real estate developers in America. Today, Memphis based Belz Enterprises owns and manages more than 25 million square feet of shopping centers, hotels, office buildings, and warehouse space. Today, Jack Belz, son of the late founder, continues to operate the company founded by his father, along with third generation family members (sons Martin Belz, Ronald Belz, and son in law Andy Groveman). They, along with other executives share responsibility for the various divisions of this large company.

# PEABODY PLACE

For nearly 40 years, since the reopening of The Peabody Hotel, Jack Belz and Belz Enterprises have been working on the project known as Peabody Place. Peabody Place, which is now open, is one of America's largest multi-use commercial developments. It is comprised of eight city blocks and contains more than 2,000,000 square feet of residential, commercial, retail, office, and entertainment space. The anchor at the north end is The Peabody Hotel itself. At the west end, at the waterfront, are the executive headquarters of AutoZone. At the south end, opposite The Peabody Hotel, and serving as the south anchor, is the new Hampton Inn and Suites. To the east is the new 1600 car garage. There are two additional garages, a 550 capacity garage on the south side of Peabody Place, and a 700 car garage under the office tower between Second St. and Main, at the corner of Peabody Place, in which the executive offices of Belz Enterprises are housed. The Peabody Place Trolley Station was built by Belz and is located in front of the magnificent Tower at Peabody Place. The trolley runs north to south along Main St. as part of a historic renovation comprising the entire block between Gayoso, Peabody Place, Main and Front Streets, renovation which now incorporates apartments, offices, retail, restaurants, grocery, and the Belz Museum of Asian and Judaic Art.

Jack Belz and his team have made Peabody Place a reality, and continue their involvement in rebuilding major areas of downtown Memphis. Meanwhile, other members of the family are expanding the company's activities in different areas and other types of development.

**Jack & Marilyn Belz admire a magnificent Chinese bronze.**

## BELZ MUSEUM OF ASIAN AND JUDIAC ART

This unique and beautiful museum and gallery originally opened on October 15, 1998 as a 7,500 square foot facility housing a wide variety of rare and exquisite Chinese artifacts and selected items from the extensive personal collection of Jack and Marilyn Belz. It has since been expanded to 24,000 square feet and now additionally includes Italian mosaics, Judaica, exotic minerals and specimens, Russian lacquered boxes, and priceless works of art from other categories. Among the many rare and one of a kind artifacts on display are exquisite Chinese lacquered chairs, delicately carved jade, agate, and ivory pieces, many of extreme antiquity. This museum is something which must be seen. One cannot help but marvel at the items on display. The intricacy and detail of some of the ivory carvings is almost beyond description.

## The Dynasty Room

Another feature of the Belz Museum is its Dynasty Room, a perfect Asian styled setting for a luncheon of up to 40 guests, or theatre seating for 50. For afternoon teas, sit down dinners, wedding receptions, or any other function in an intimate setting. With available outdoor gallery, entry hall, and lobby there is a total space suitable for 400, for a reception or cocktail party.

**1916 Hotel Envelope Corner**

The museum is located in the Pembroke Building at 119 South Main and is within easy walking distance of The Peabody. It is open daily except Monday.

Phone: 901-523-2787

Website: Belzmuseum.org

Information: info@belzmuseum.org

**Bernard Lansky, `Clothier to the King.'**

Anybody who knows anything about Elvis Presley knows that a large part of his style came from the clothes he bought at Lansky Brothers on Beale Street. Lansky Bros. catered to a large number of predominantly black Beale Street and Memphis entertainers in the post World War II era. Elvis Presley, heavily influenced by their stylish clothes as well as their roots music, sought to emulate their appearance as well as sound. While it is well known that Lansky Brothers were influential in the development of his early signature style, what is not generally known is that Bernard Lansky designed and tailored many of Elvis' most famous stage costumes as well as most of his daily wear throughout his career. Bernard Lansky was seldom seen without his measuring tape draped around his neck, and is fondly remembered by anyone who knew him. His lasting influence on American, and consequently world fashion and culture is every bit as significant as that of any of the great New York, Los Angeles, Paris, or London designers who succeeded him in their respective fields.

**Lansky at The Peabody**, featuring Fine Men's sportswear. The Lansky family name in Memphis has long been synonymous with cutting edge fashions for more than 72 years. In fact it was Lansky Brothers on Beale Street where Elvis Presley shopped for many of his most distinctive clothes. This famous shop, now located in The Peabody Hotel lobby, features the very latest in men's fashions from some of the world's foremost brands and designers. Lansky Brothers also designs an exclusive fashion label called 'Lansky Brothers, Clothier to the King.' You are always welcome to shop or browse through their many wonderful clothing selections. And while you're there, don't forget to look up, and enjoy the large collection of guitars adorning the walls autographed by the many famous musicians who have shopped at Lansky at The Peabody. 901-529 9070

**Lansky 126-Clothes That Rock** for men and women. Lansky 126 is a trend setting contemporary boutique for men and women with all the latest styles in clothing, accessories, and footwear.

store. 901-405-7625, or on line:

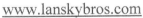
www.lanskybros.com

**The Lucky Duck**

**The Lucky Duck** is the perfect gift shop with anything and everything having to do with ducks! This exciting shop is located in the hotel lobby right next door to the elevator that each day transports the famous Peabody Ducks to and from the magnificent marble fountain where they pass their days pleasantly swimming around the centerpiece. In answer to the constant demand for Peabody souvenirs, The Lucky Duck is stocked with a wide variety of top brand name merchandise emblazoned with the distinctive Peabody Hotel logo. From beautiful Turkish robes, and one of a kind wooden ducks, to coffee mugs, sleep shirts, and 'Legend of the Duck' T-shirts, and duck items of all types, there is something for everyone.

A great selection of merchandise is also available for children, including plush stuffed ducks, infant wear, toys and children's books which feature the story of the famous Peabody Ducks. The finest in gifts and souvenirs is also available including Swarovski Crystal, Lladro Figurines, Christopher Radko Ornaments, and many more. 901-432-0943,

Shop on line: www.peabodyducks.com

**LANSKY THE ACCESSORIES SHOP** For ladies, showcases unique jewelry, handbags, scarves, and apparel, in an exquisite environment. 901-844-1933

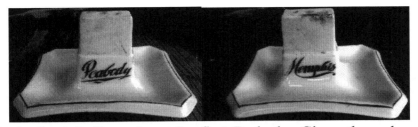

**Peabody Ash Tray** from the first Peabody. Given the red and white color of this ash tray-match striker, it's most likely from 1915 or thereabouts, and probably from German company Bauscher which made the egg cup shown at the bottom of page 27.

## ACKNOWLEDGEMENTS

Special thanks to Jack Belz for proofreading the manuscript, to Judy Wesley, who kindly and graciously granted us access to everything we needed. Patricia LaPointe of the Memphis & Shelby County Room at the Memphis-Shelby County Public Library on Poplar; and to her husband Jack McFarland, chief architect of The Peabody's restoration. Thanks also to Kelly Earnest, Director of Marketing, The Peabody; Jack Thomas, Maribel Imbaguingo, and Duckmaster Doug Weatherford, The Peabody. Thanks also to The Peabody for supplying many of the images used, and Heff Gaudino, Belz Enterprises. Special thanks to Henry Juszkiewicz at Gibson USA, makers of the world's finest guitars, basses, and mandolins. The Lucille' plant and the Smithsonian's Memphis Rock n' Soul Museum in the Beale Street Entertainment District. Thanks also to Hal, Bernard, and Julie Lansky, `Clothiers to The King,' who initially suggested this project; Chad Selden; Clay Yager; Kingsley Hooker; Bard and W. Selden; Steve & Beth Crump.

Also by **SCOTT FARAGHER**

**Music City Babylon, Inside the World of Country Music**-Birch Lane, New York, 1992

**The Branson, Missouri Scrapbook**-Citadel. New York, 1994

**The Complete Guide to Riverboat Gambling**-Citadel. New York, 1994

**Making it in Country Music**-Citadel. New York, 1996

**Nashville, Gateway to the South**-Cumberland House. Nashville, 1998

**New Orleans (Postcard History Series**)-Arcadia. Charleston, SC., 1999

**Nashville in Vintage Postcards-Arcadia**. Charleston, SC., 1999

**Memphis in Vintage Postcards** - (With Katherine Harrington) - Arcadia. Charleston, SC., 2000

**Beer Signs for the Collector**-Schiffer. Atglen, PA., 2001

**Chattanooga, Best of the Lookout City**-Milton. Chattanooga, TN.

**Cameras for the Collector**-Schiffer. Atglen, PA., 2002

**The New South** (contributing author)-Insight Guides. London, 2004

**Porsche, the Ultimate Guide**-KP Books. Iola, WI., 2005

**The Peabody Hotel** - (With Katherine Harrington) - Arcadia, Charleston, SC., 2006

**The Hammond Organ**-Scott Faragher. Nashville, 2009

**The Hammond Organ**-Hal Leonard. Milwaukee, WI., 2011

**The Arlington Resort Hotel & Spa**-(With Katherine Harrington)-Deathcat Media. Nashville, 2017

**Vignettes From the Modern Era**-Deathcat Media. Nashville, 2017

**The Pigeon Drop**-Deathcat Media. Nashville, 2017

Made in the USA
Middletown, DE
31 December 2018